Coloring Books for Grownups

DAY OF THE DEAD
PUPPIES

VISIT TODAY
ILoveColoringBooksForAdults.com
TO WIN A SET OF PREMIUM COLORED PENCILS

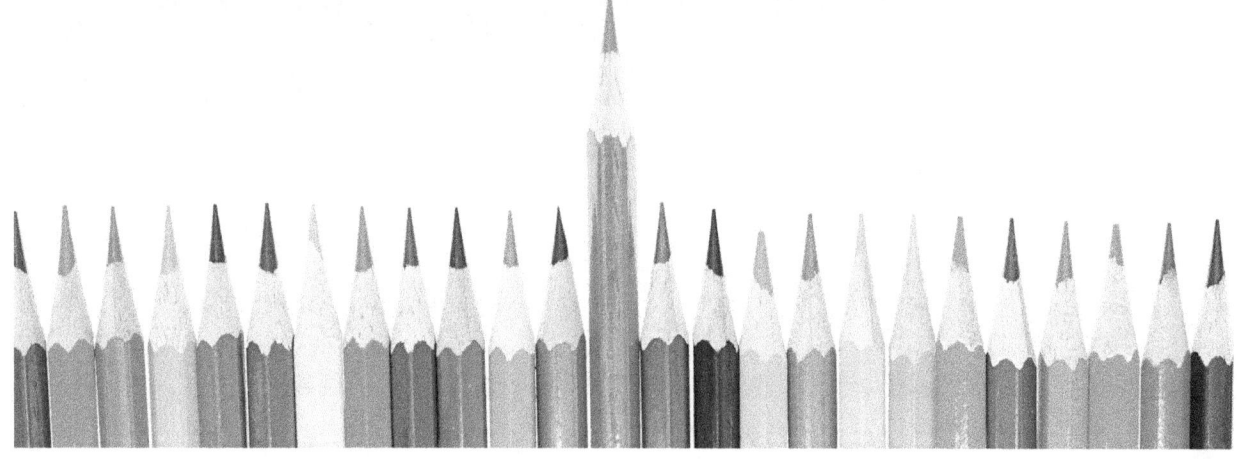

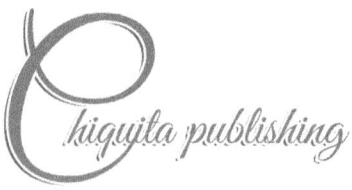
Chiquita publishing

Cover and page design by Cool Journals Studios - Copyright 2016

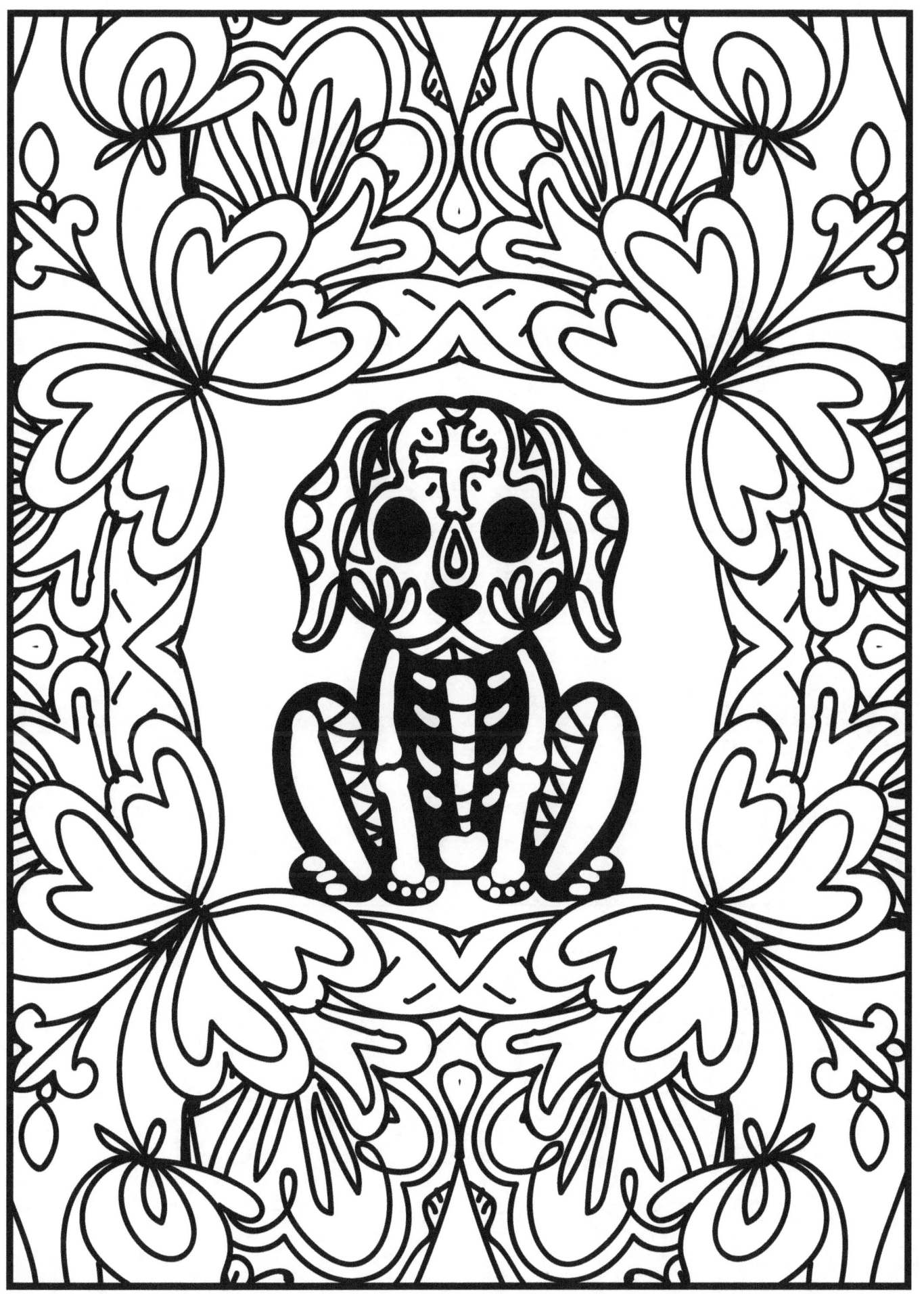

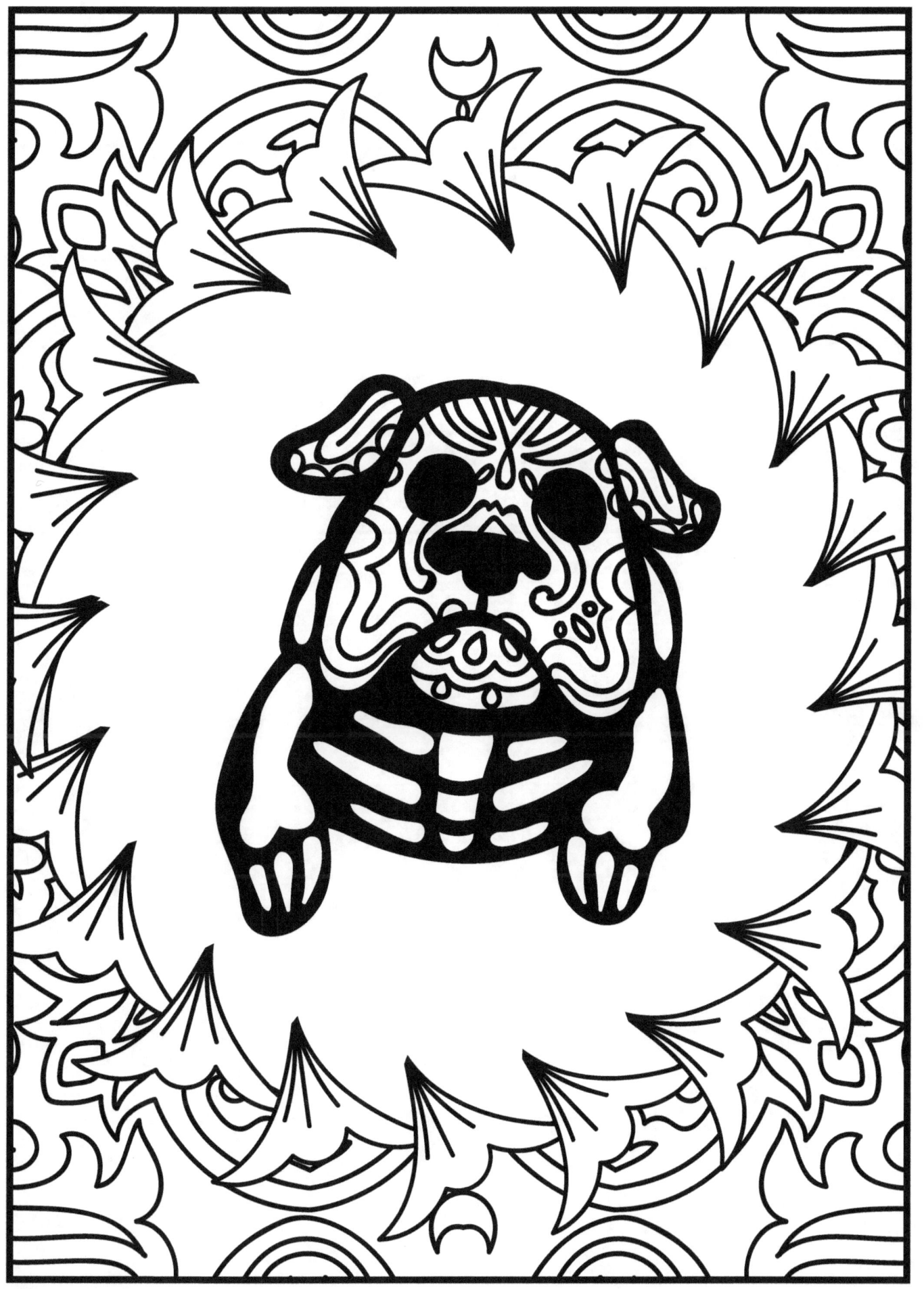

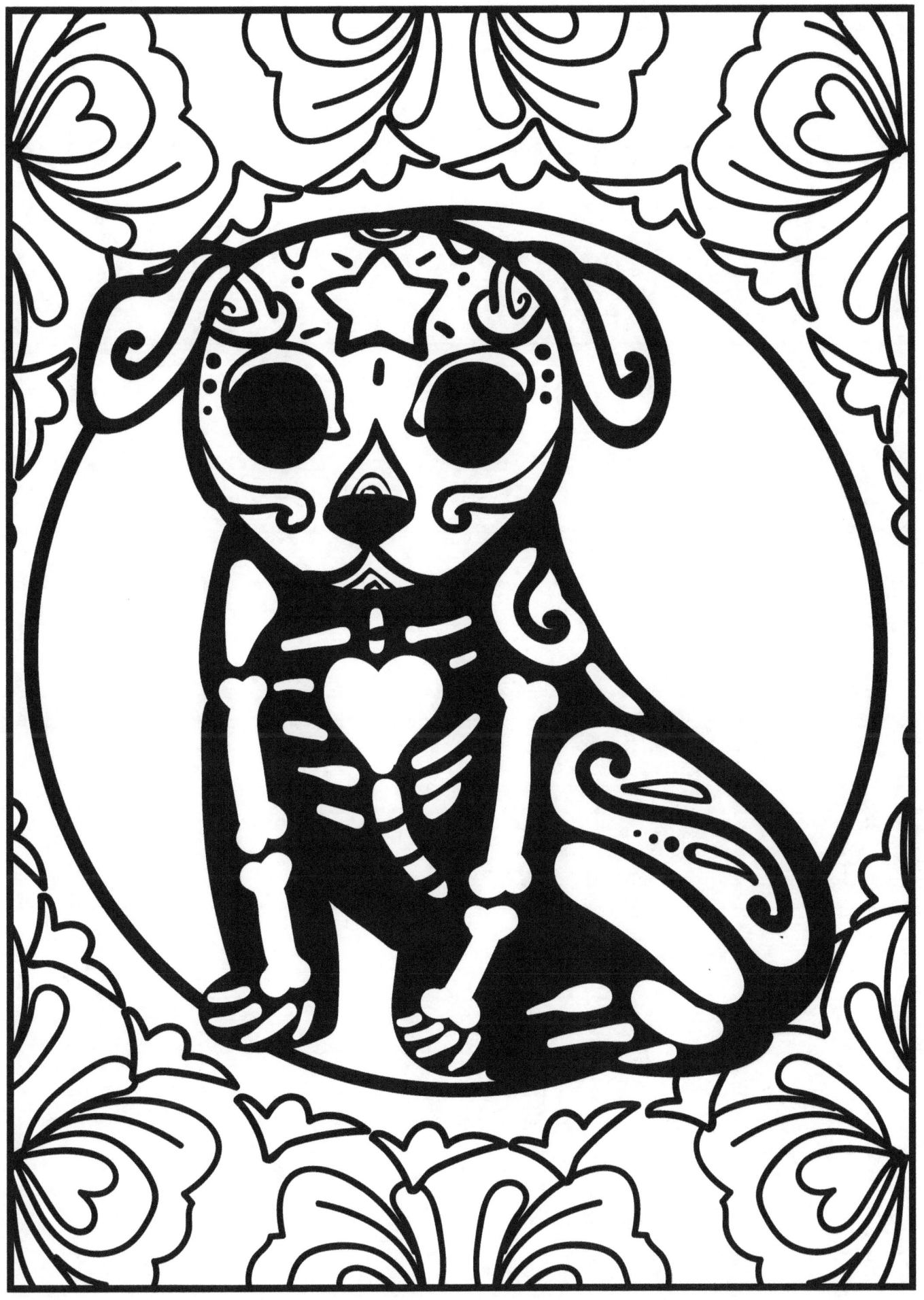

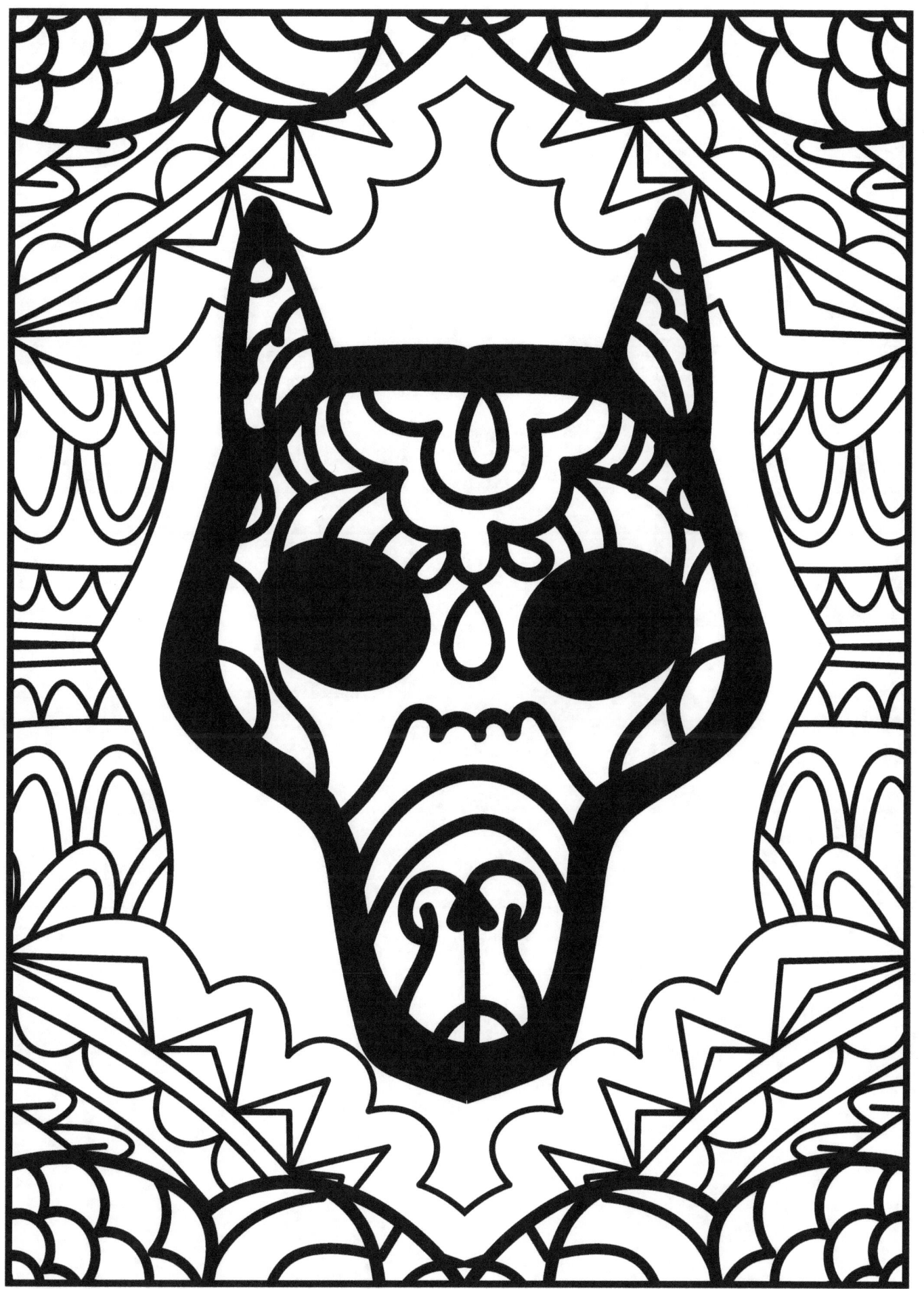

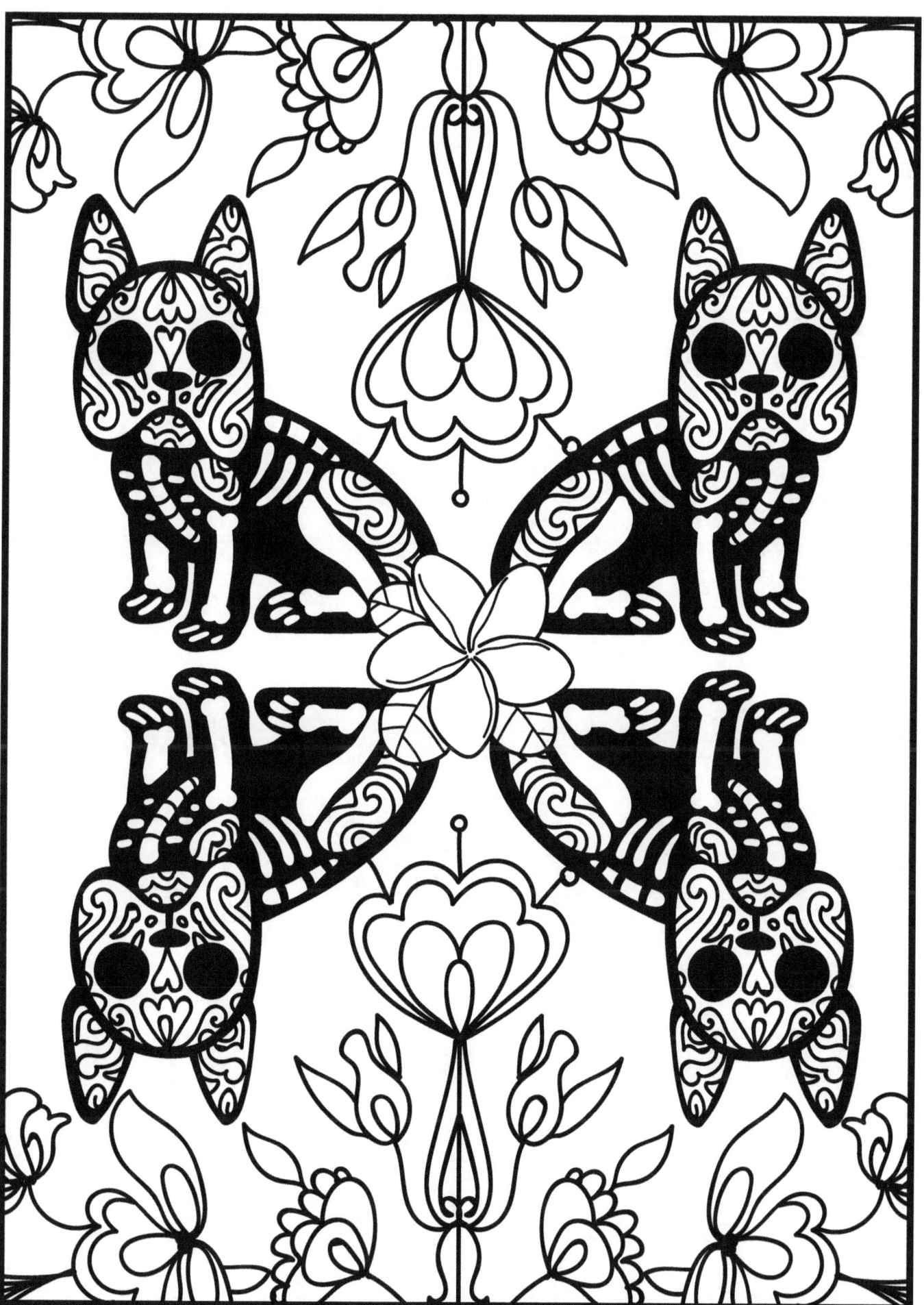

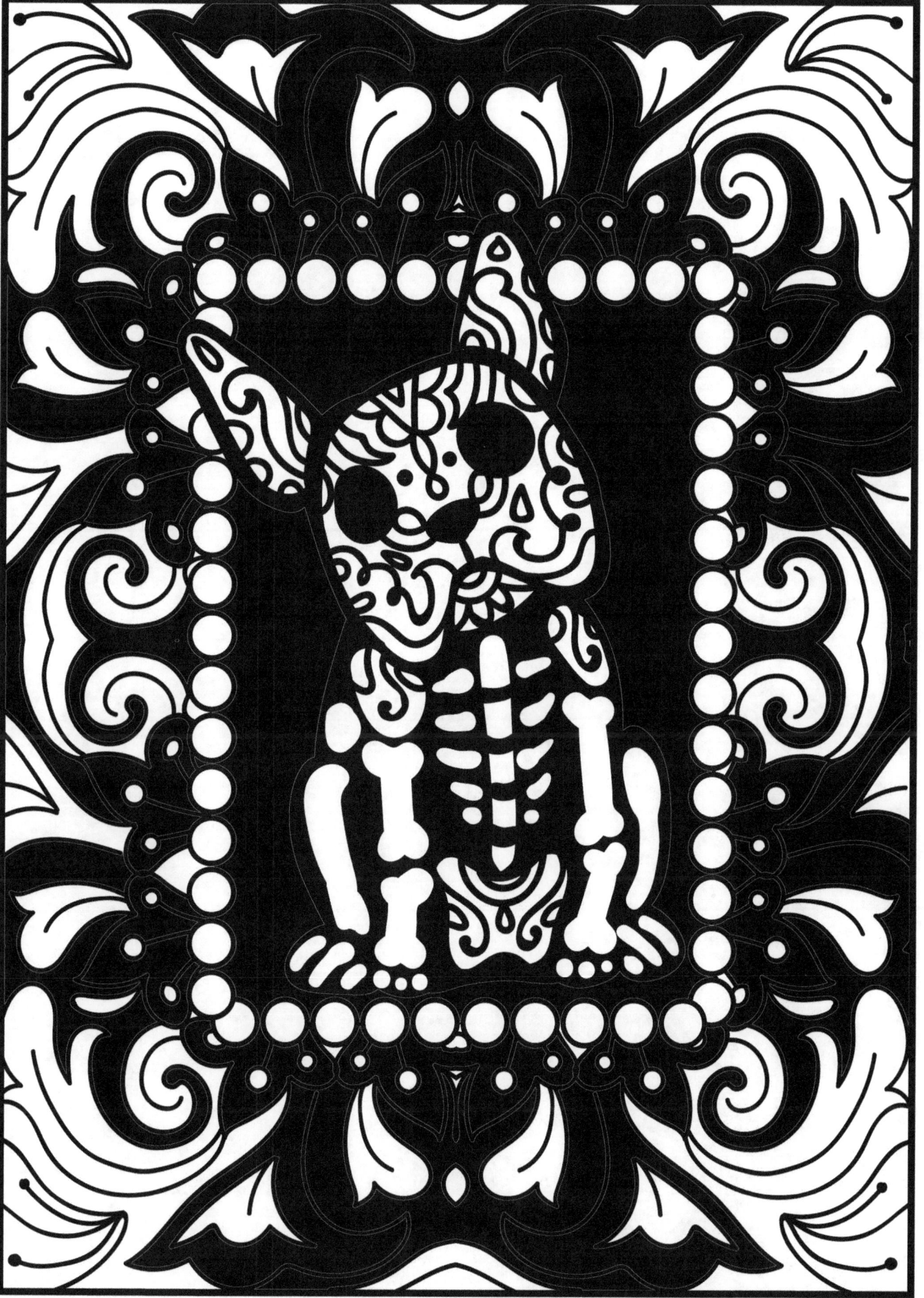

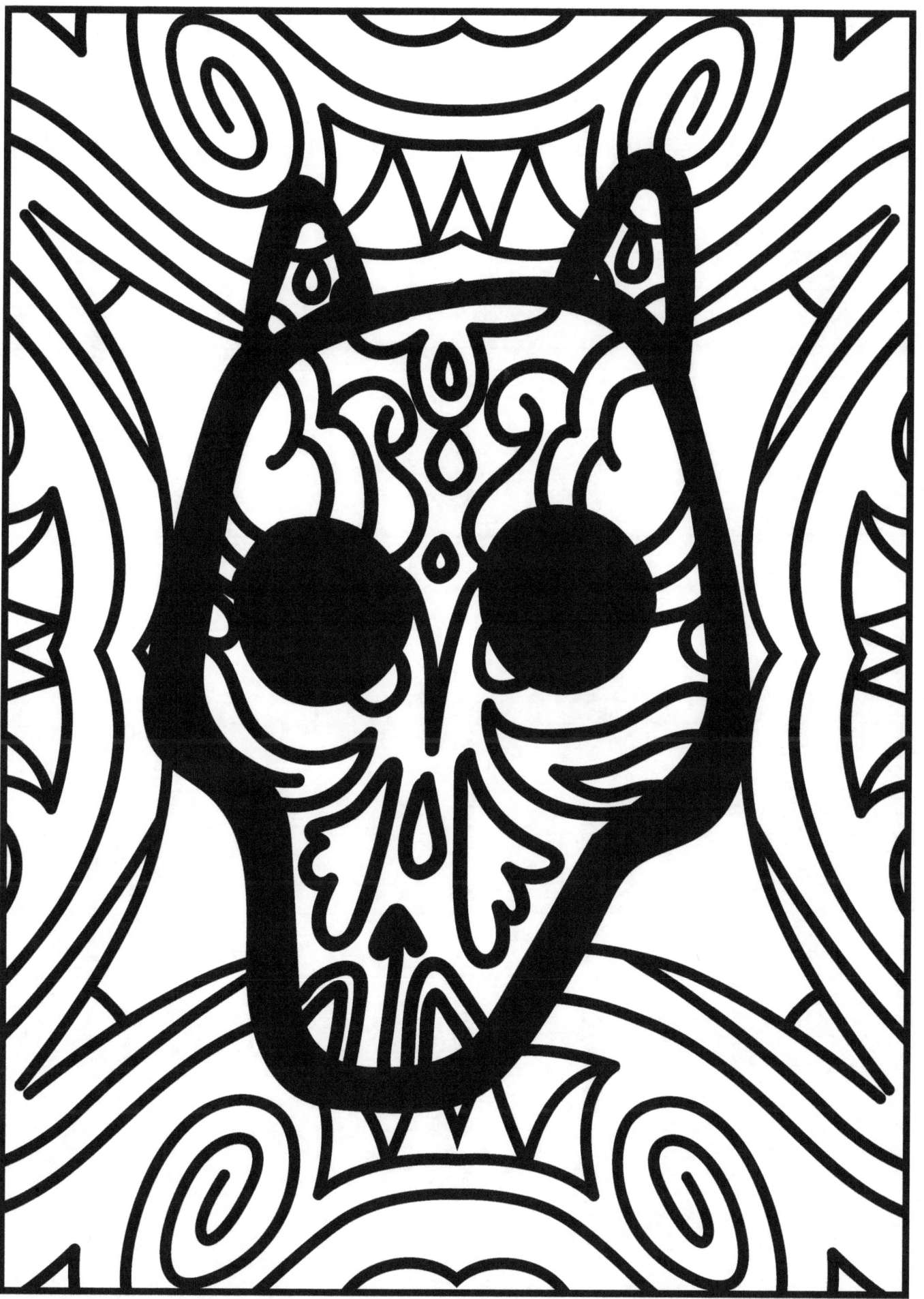

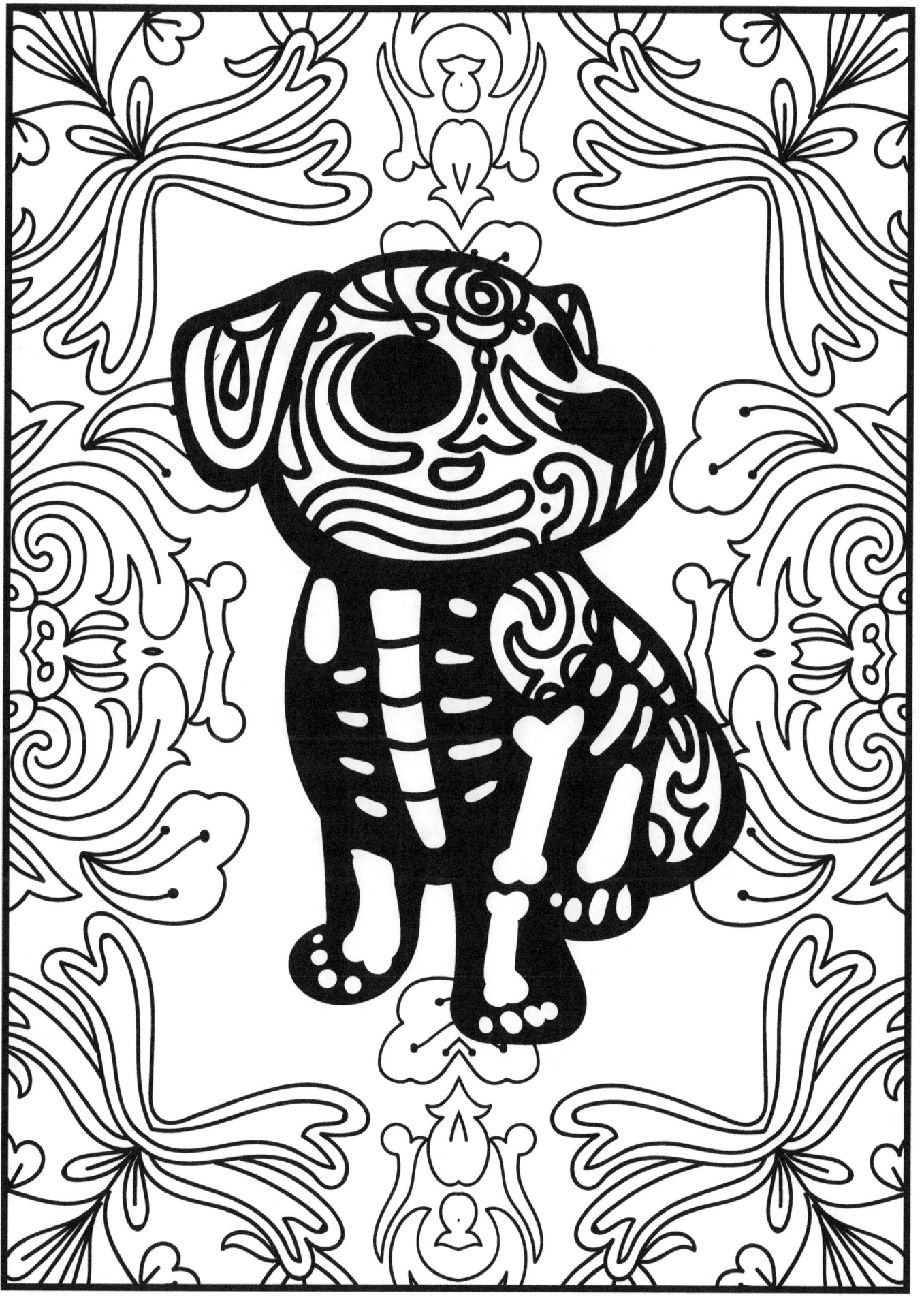

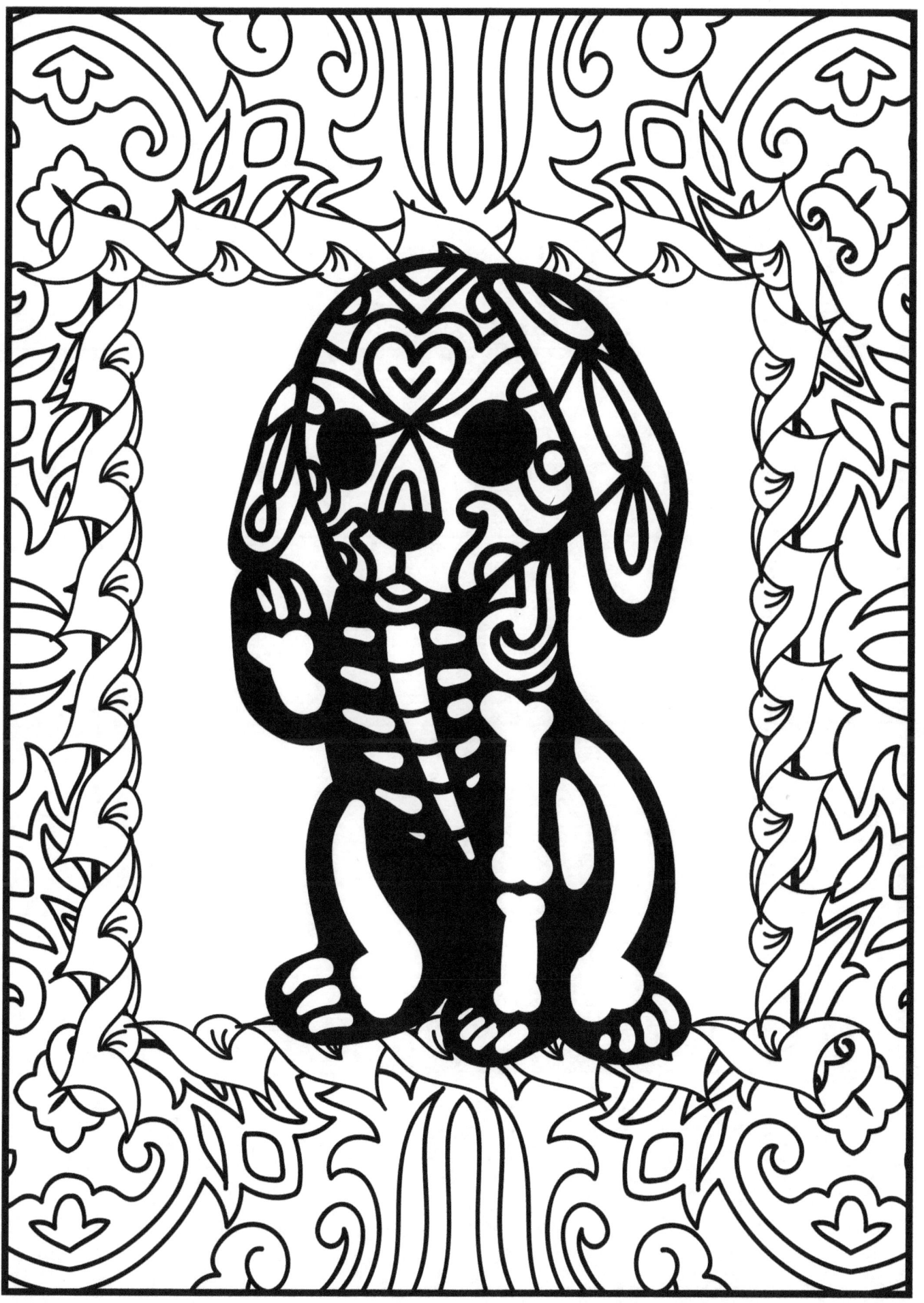

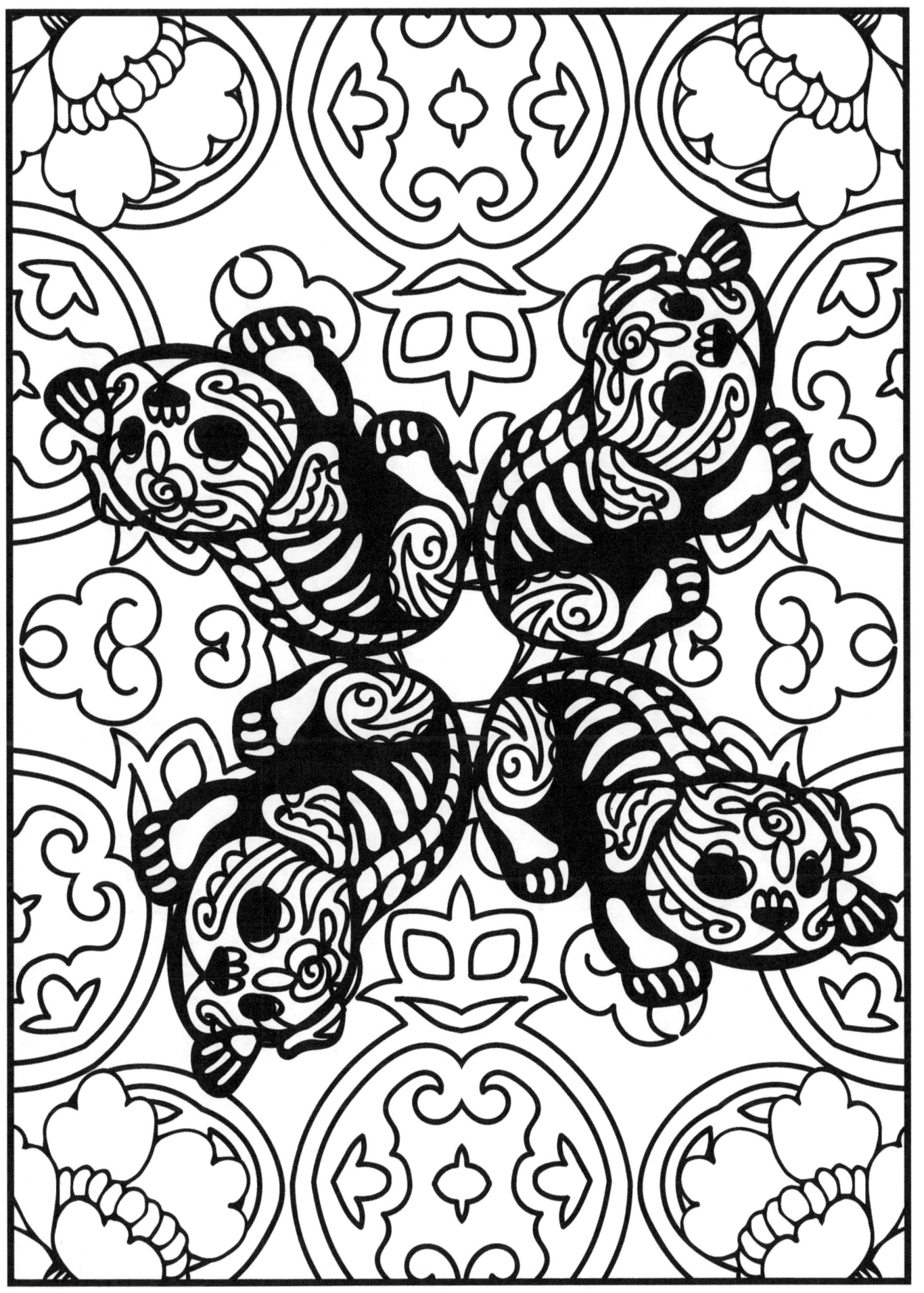

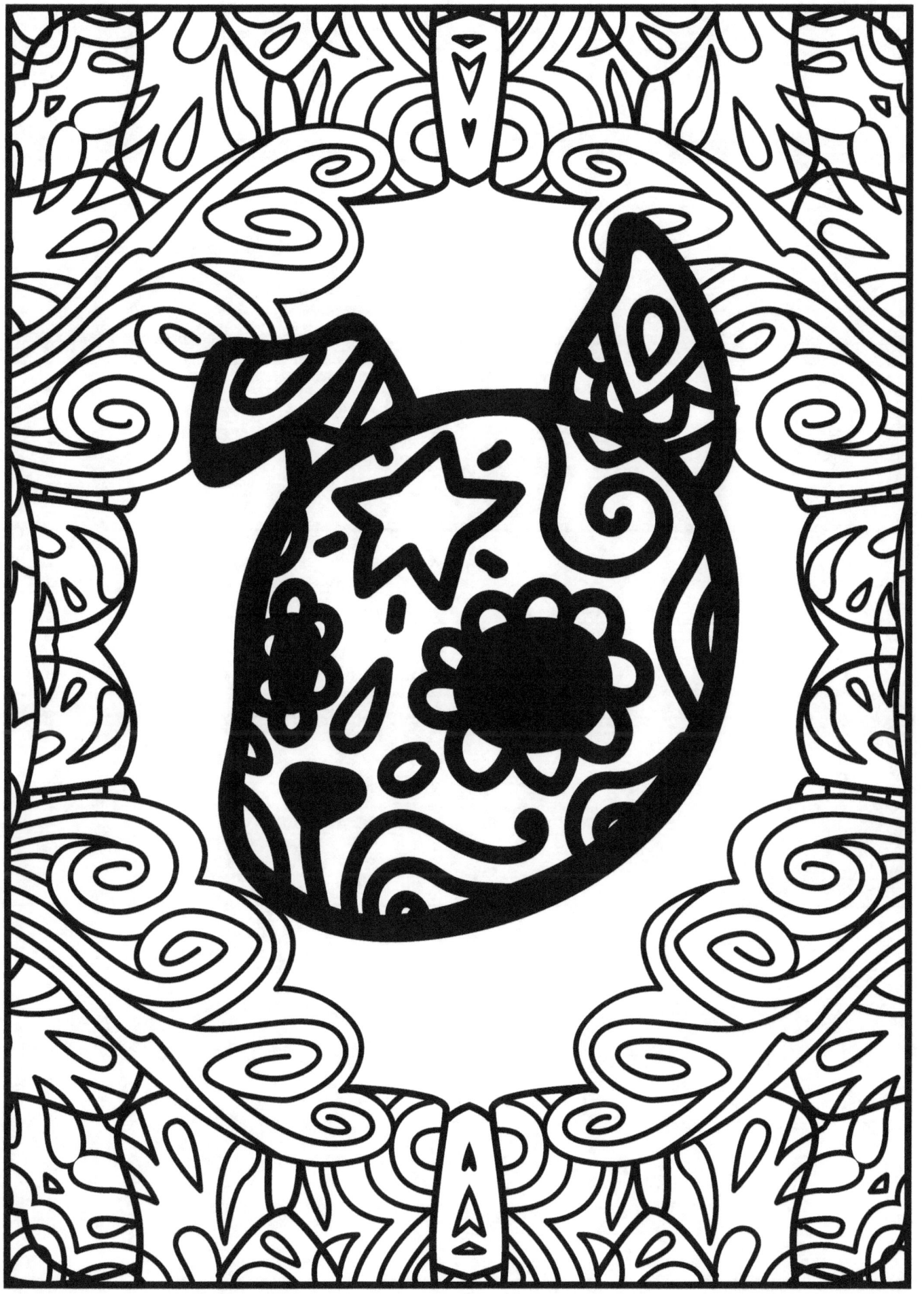

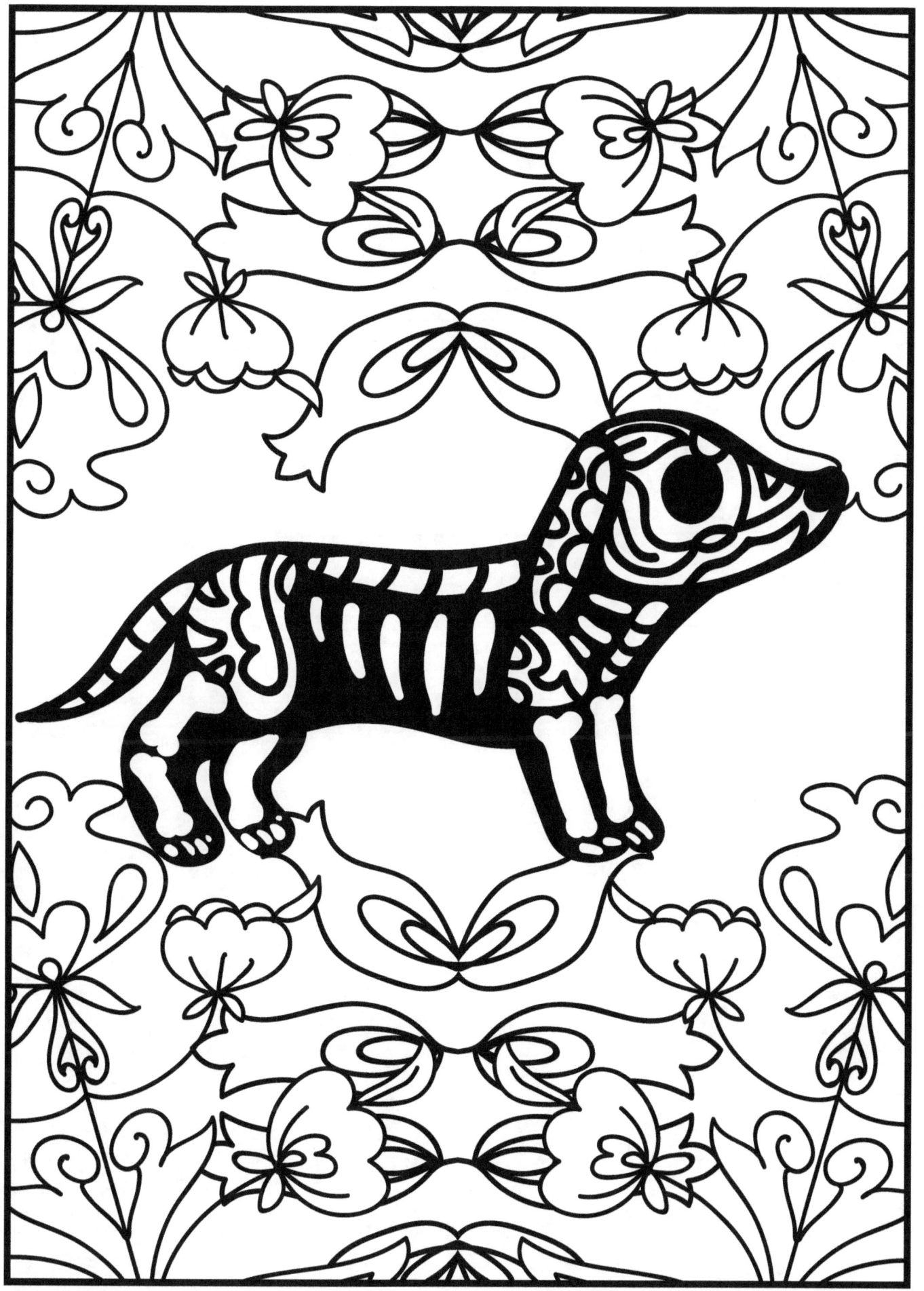

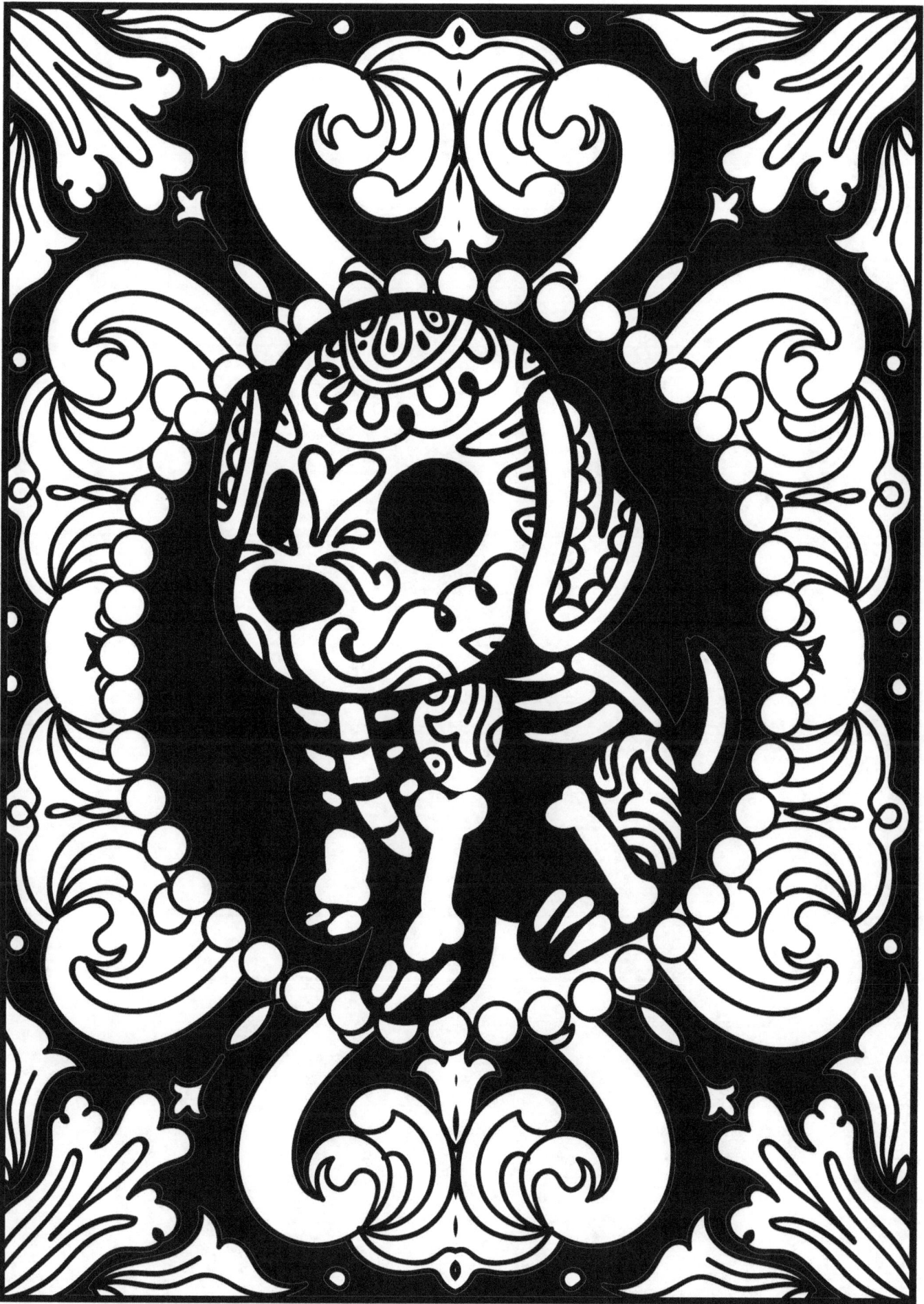

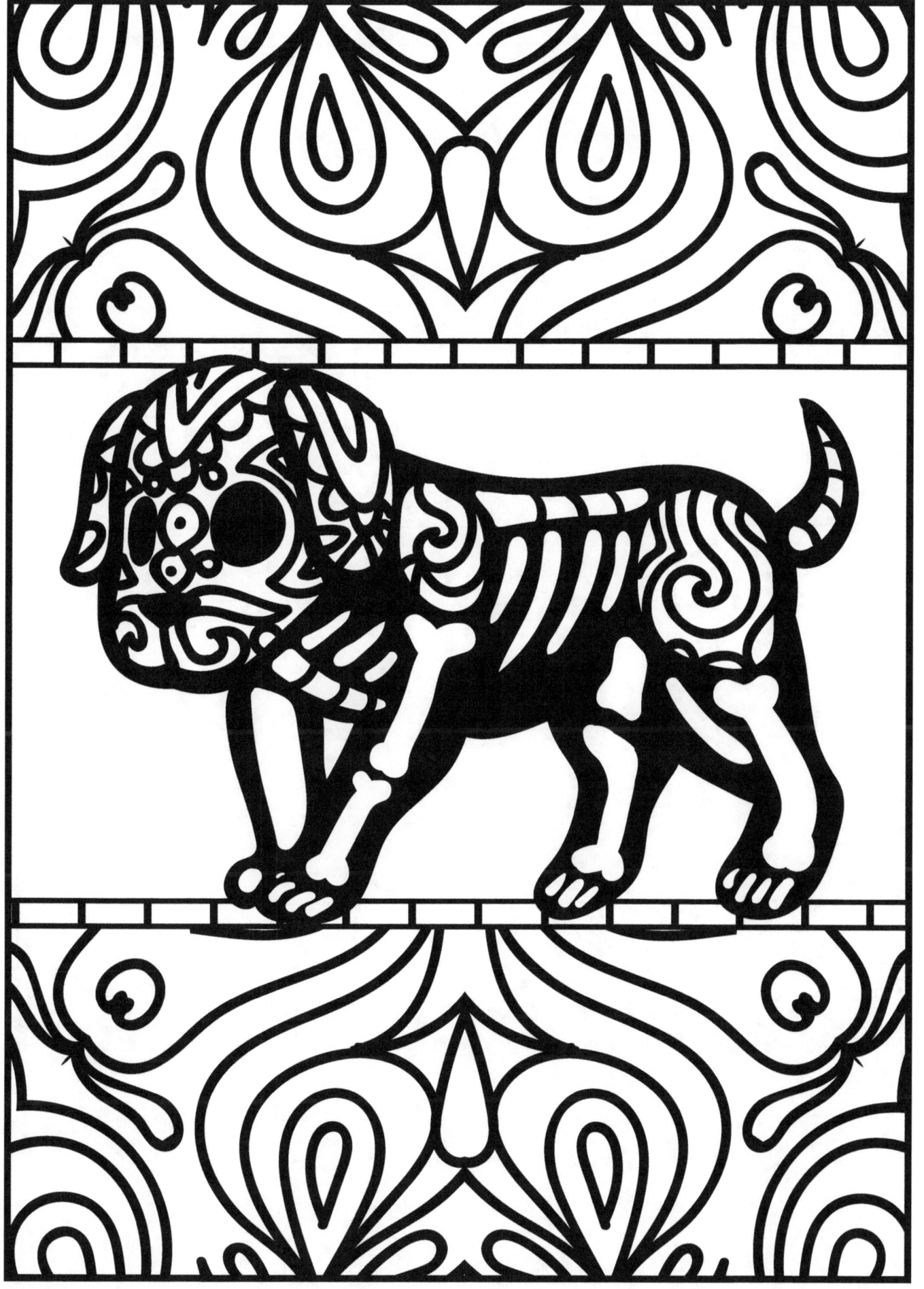

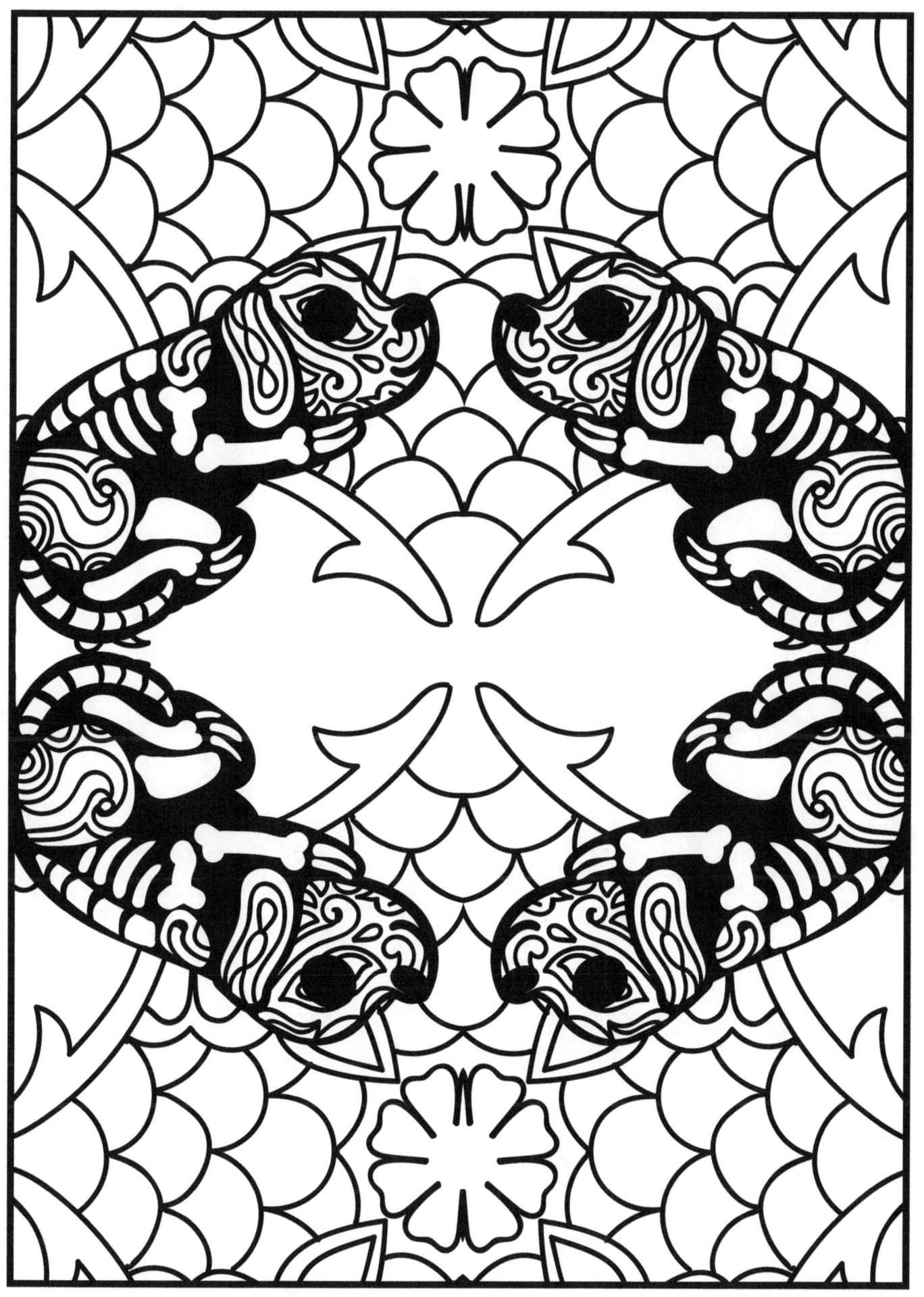

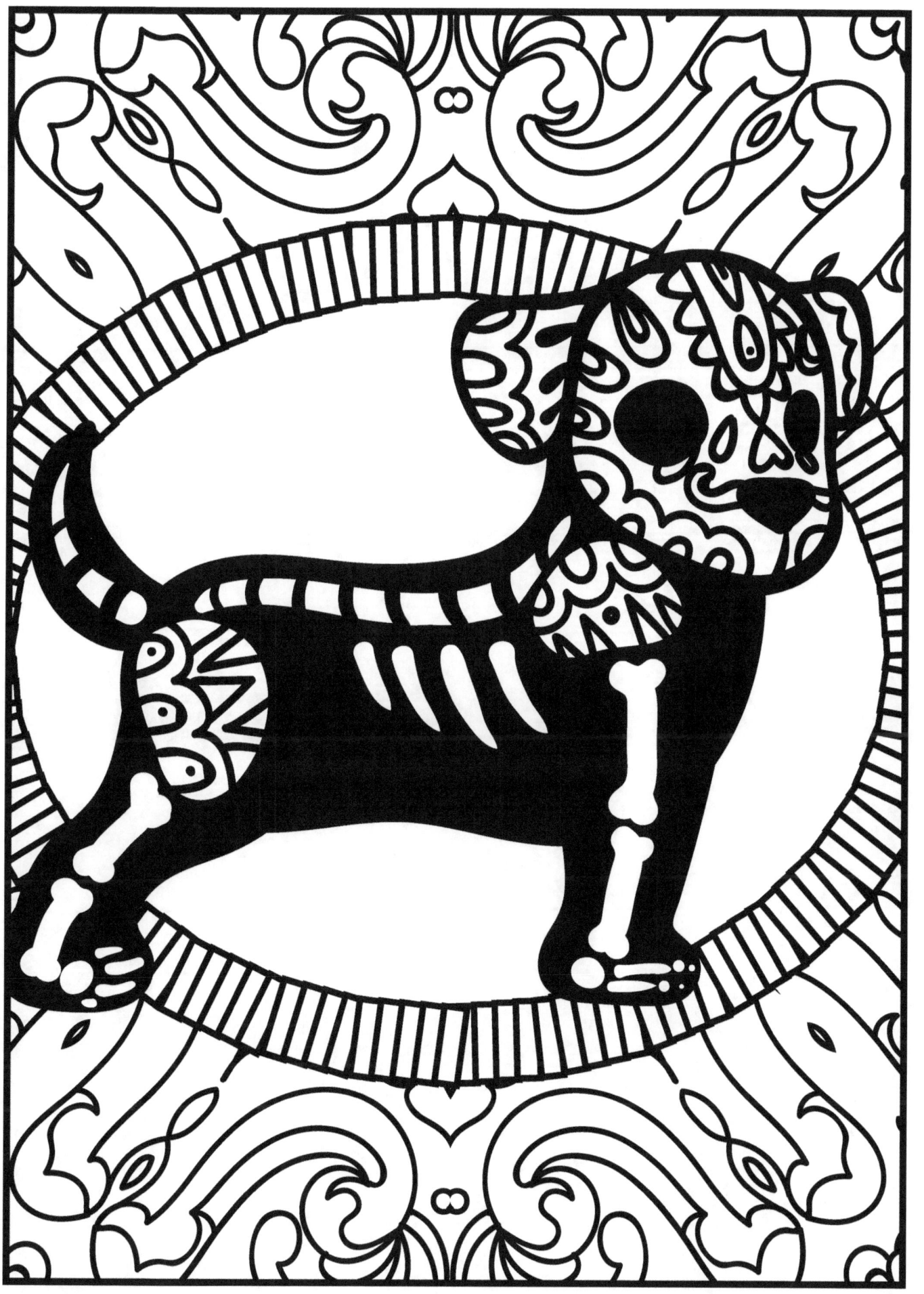

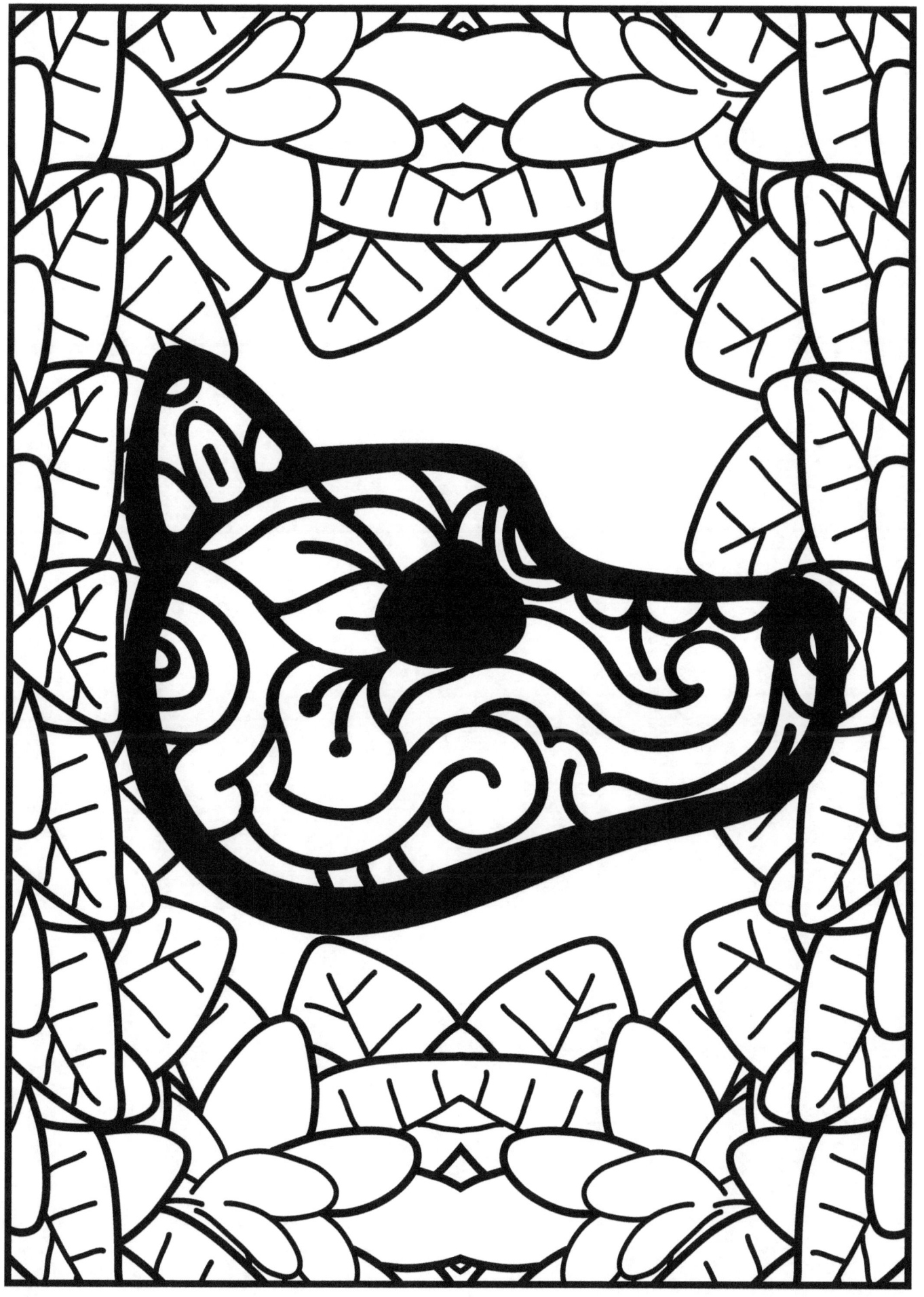

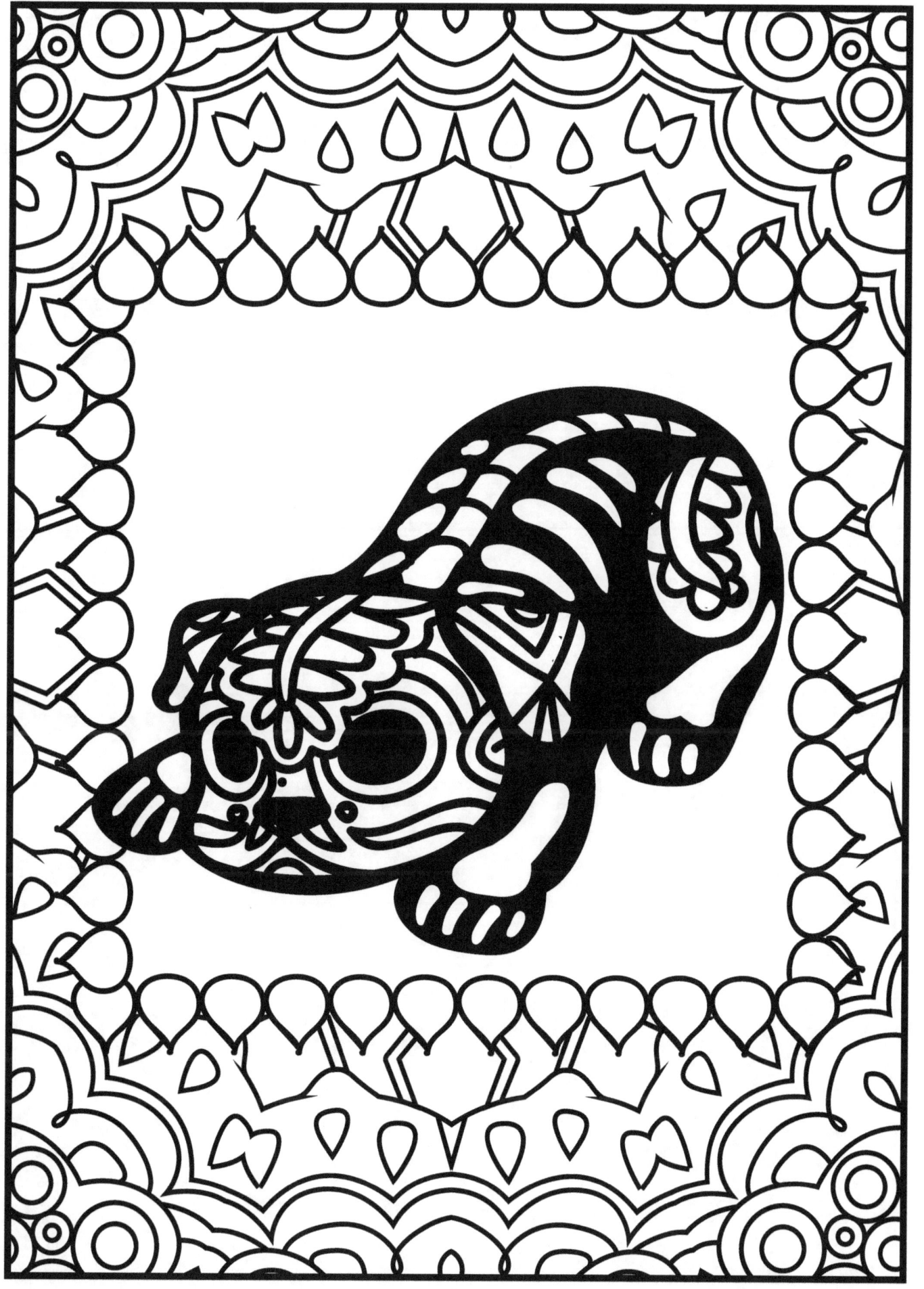

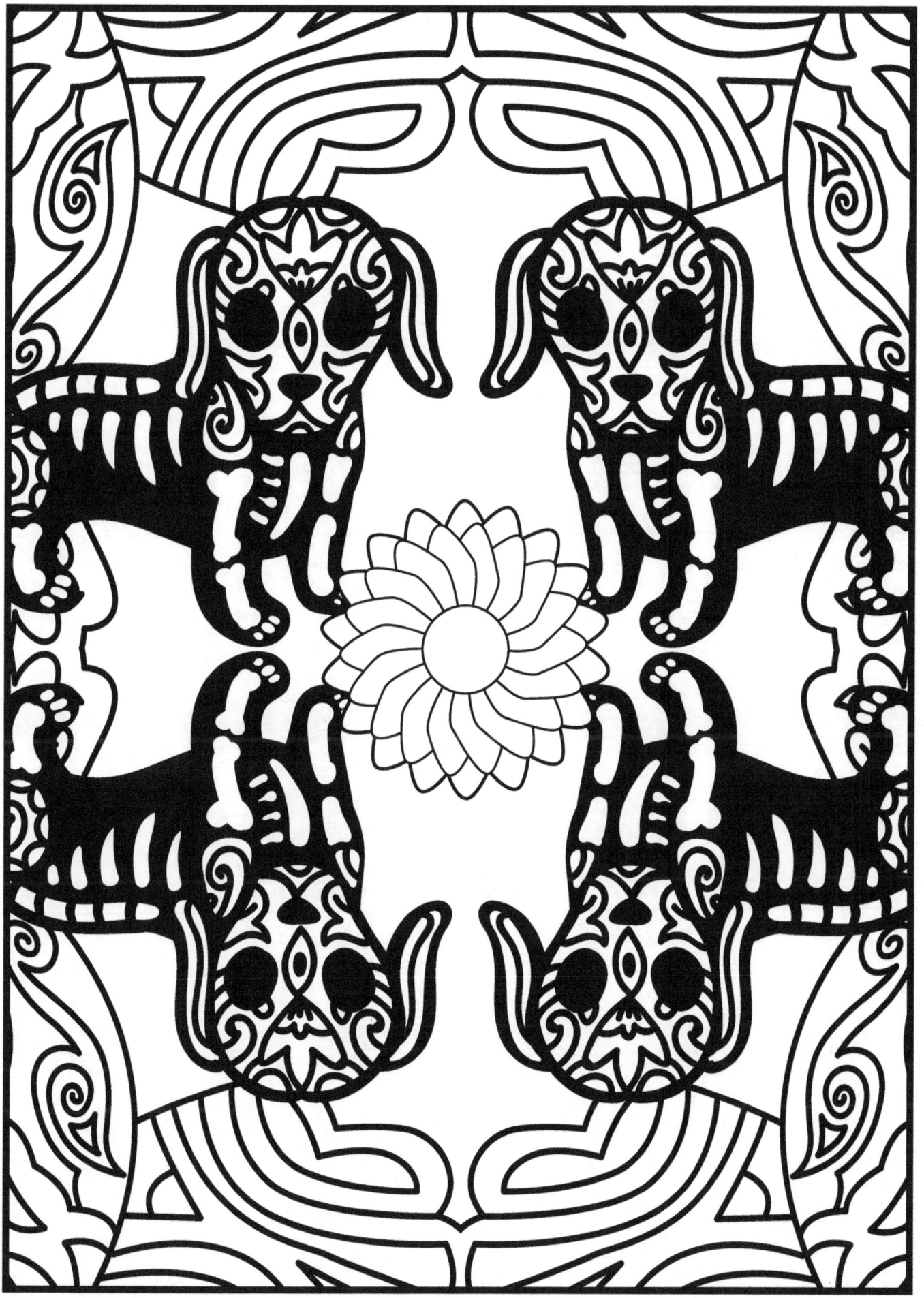

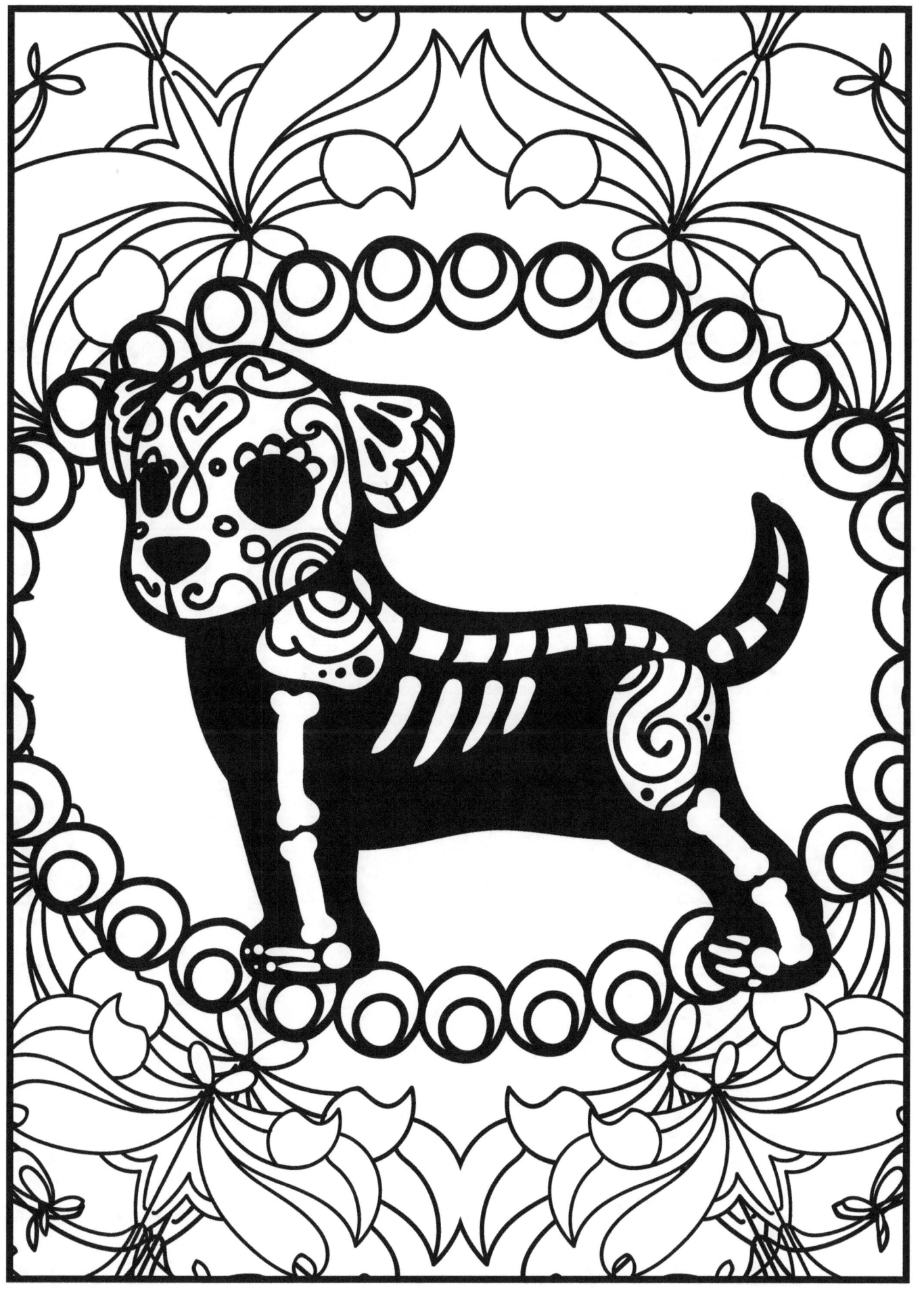

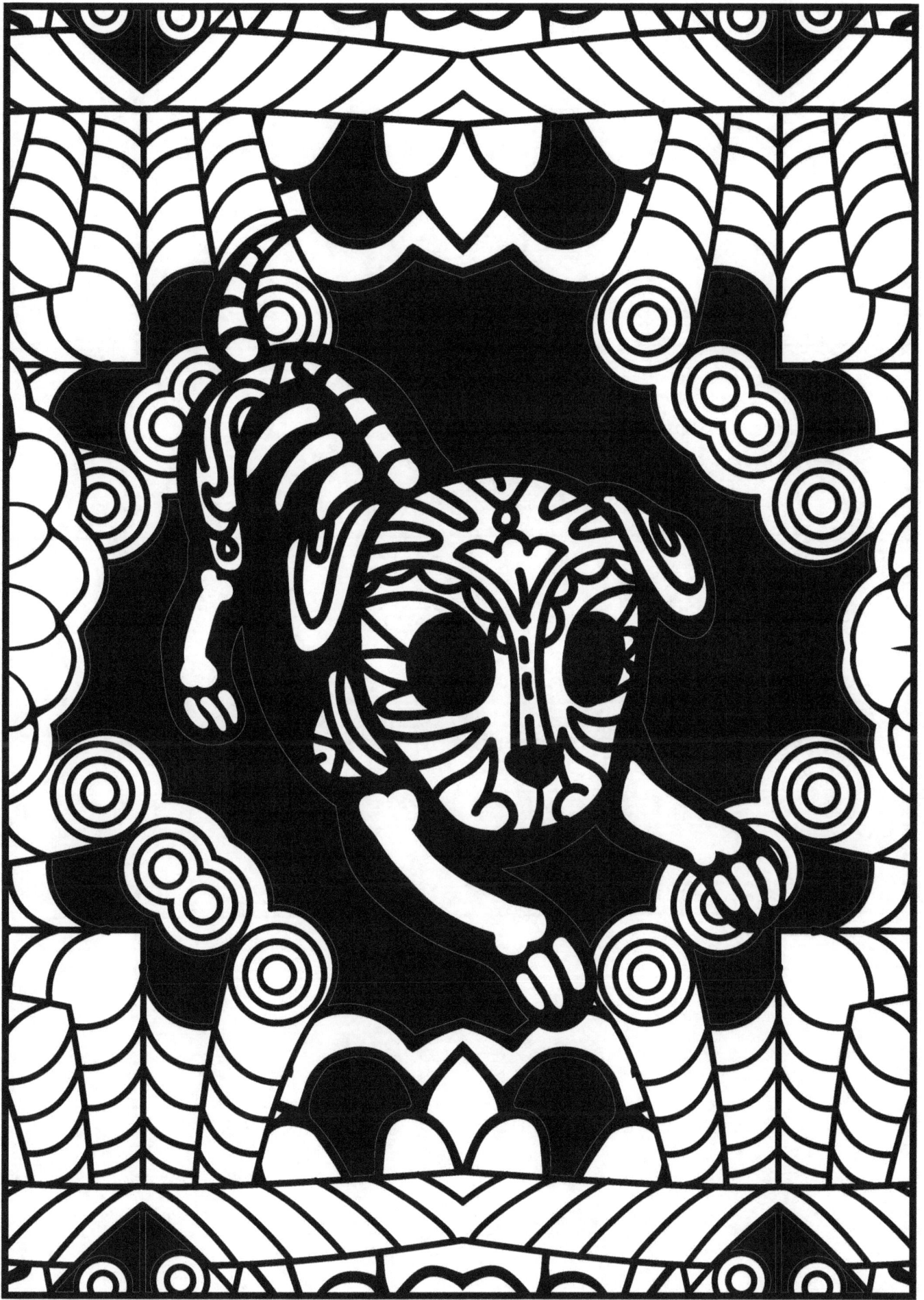

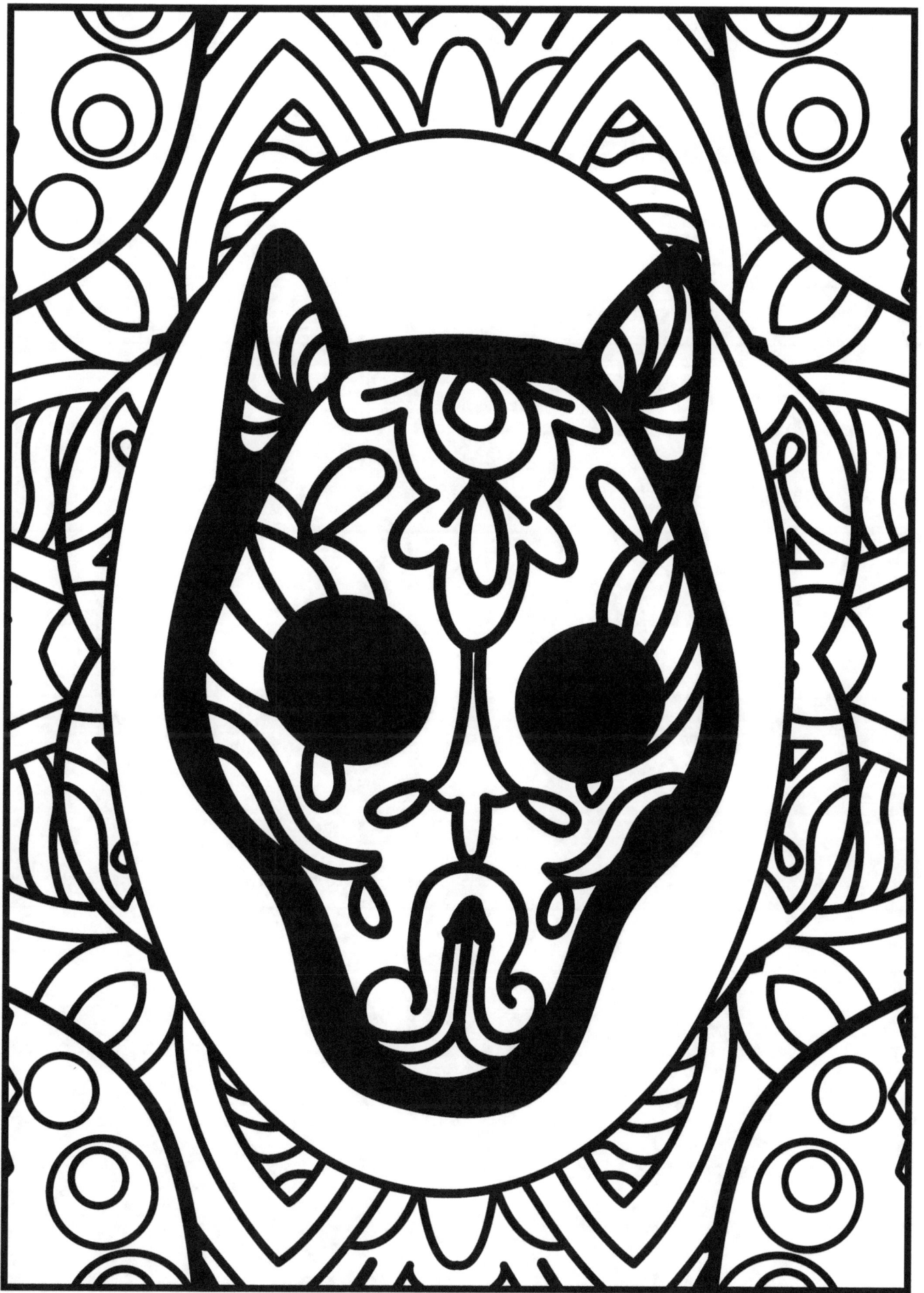

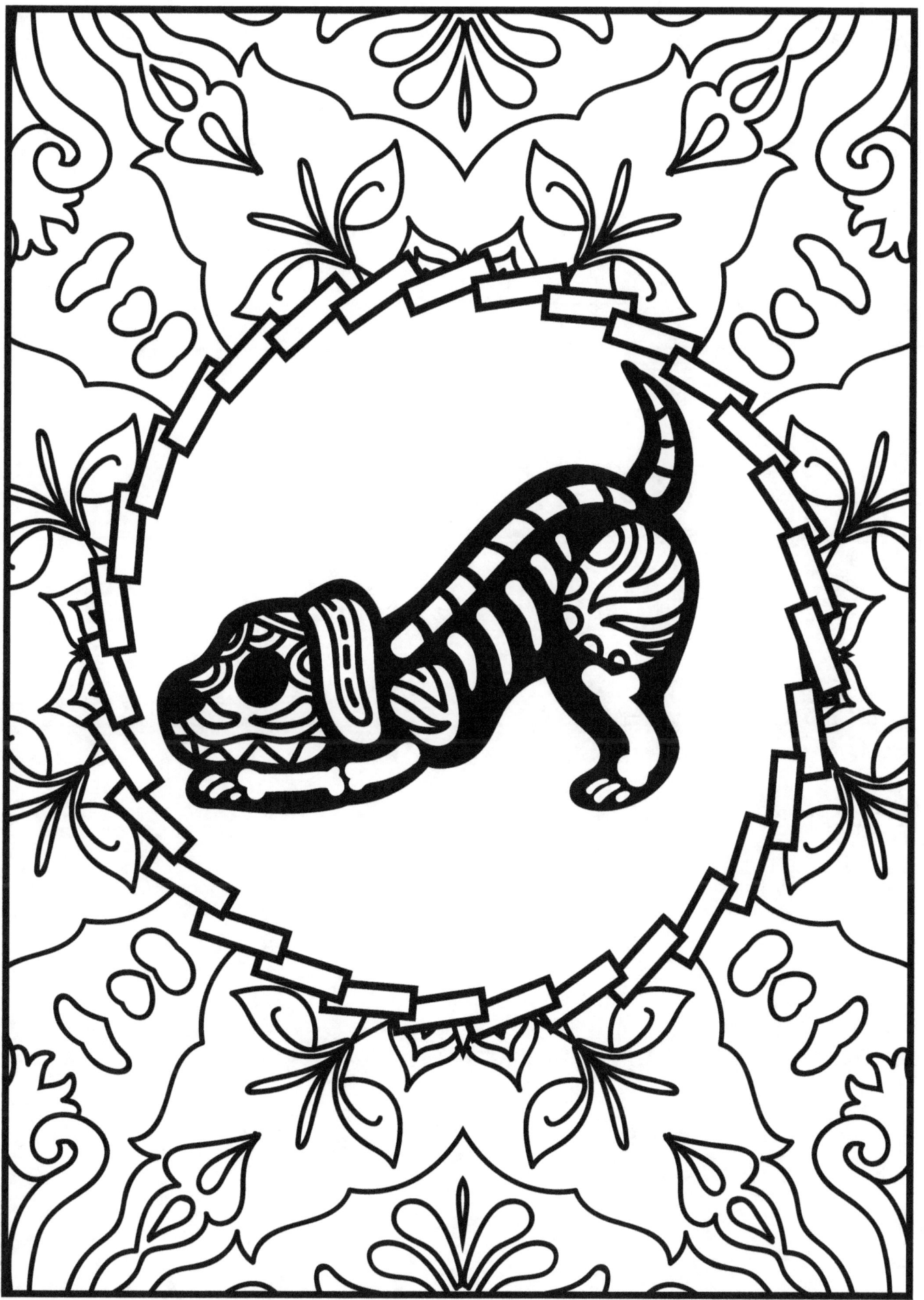

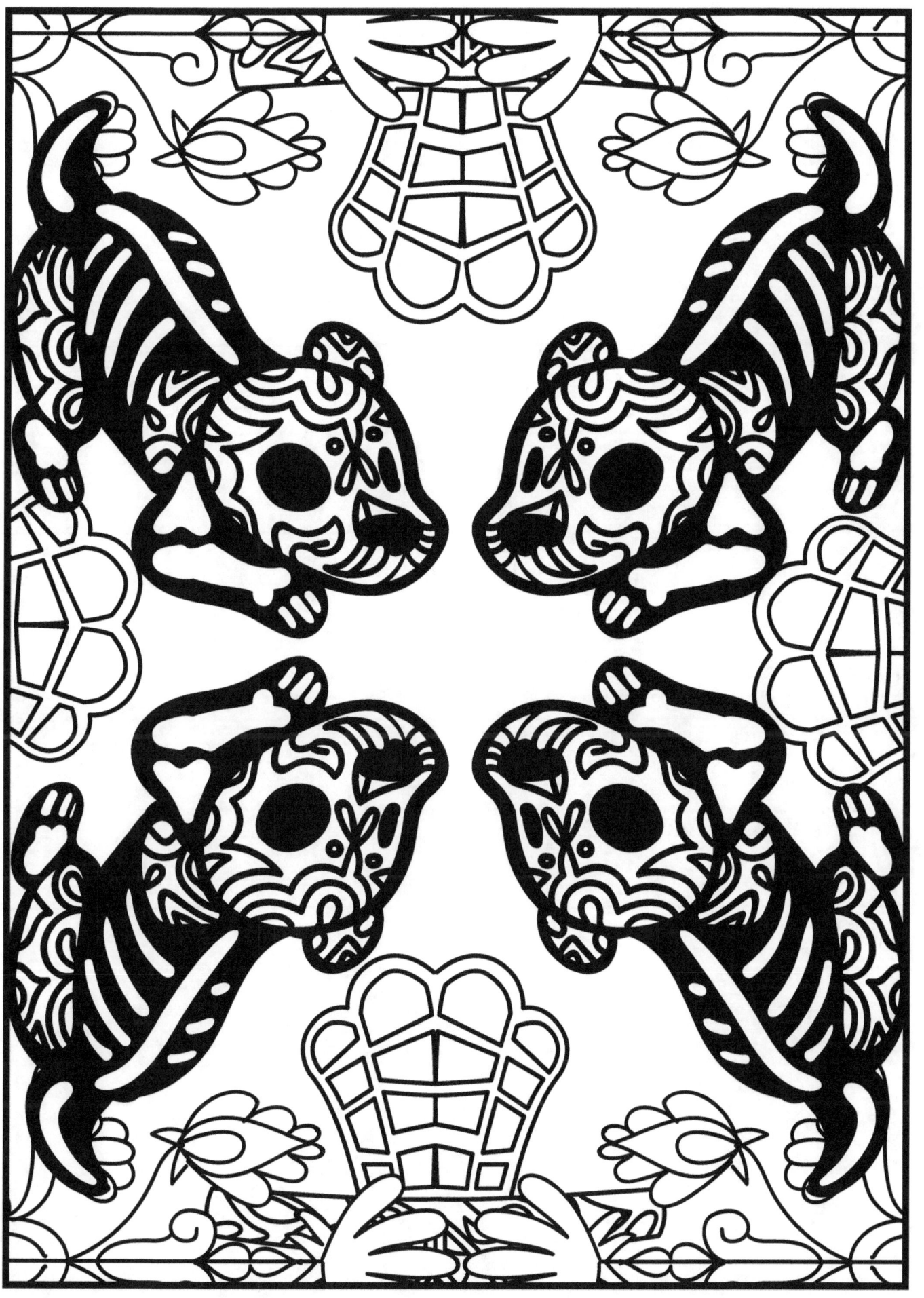

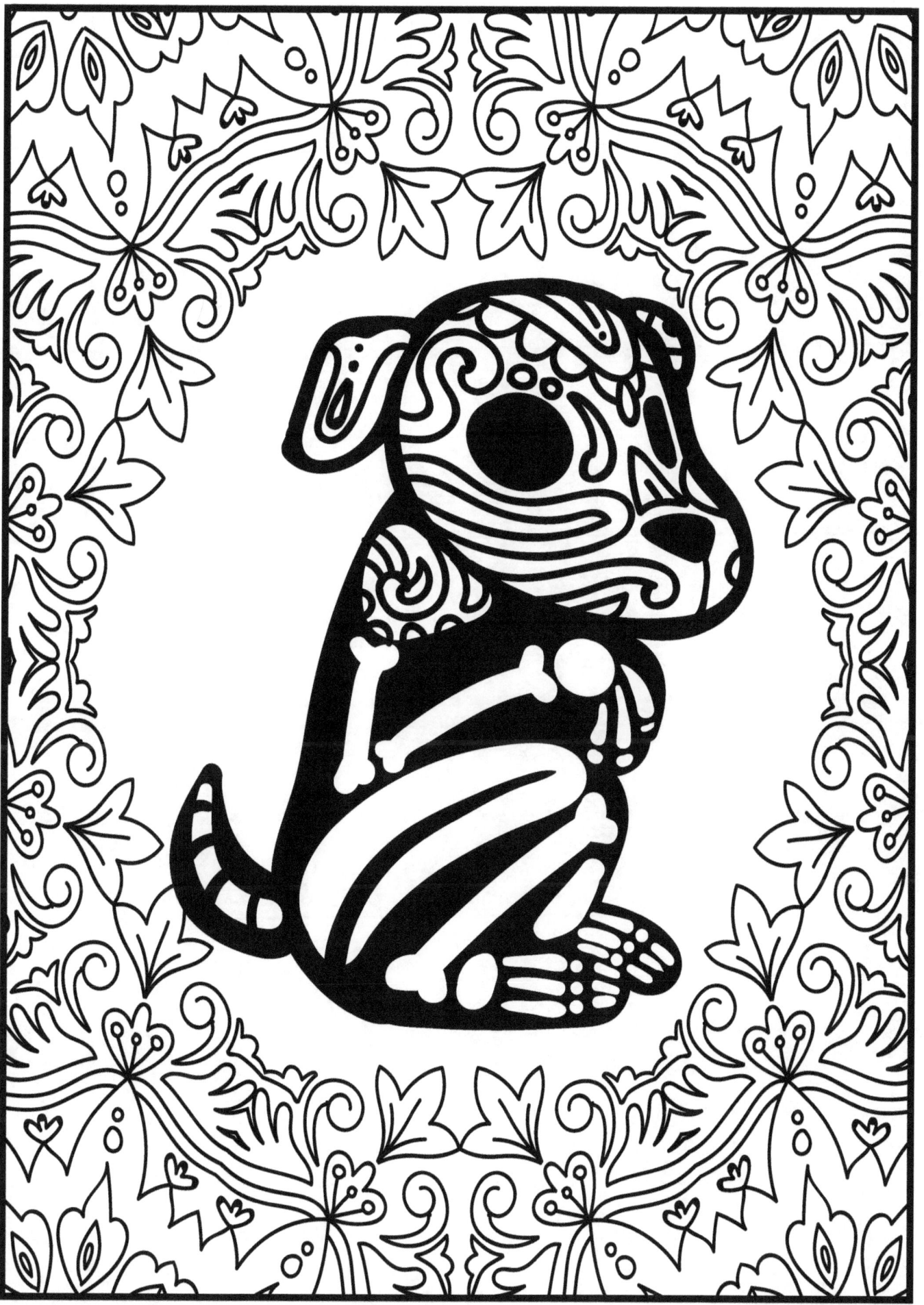

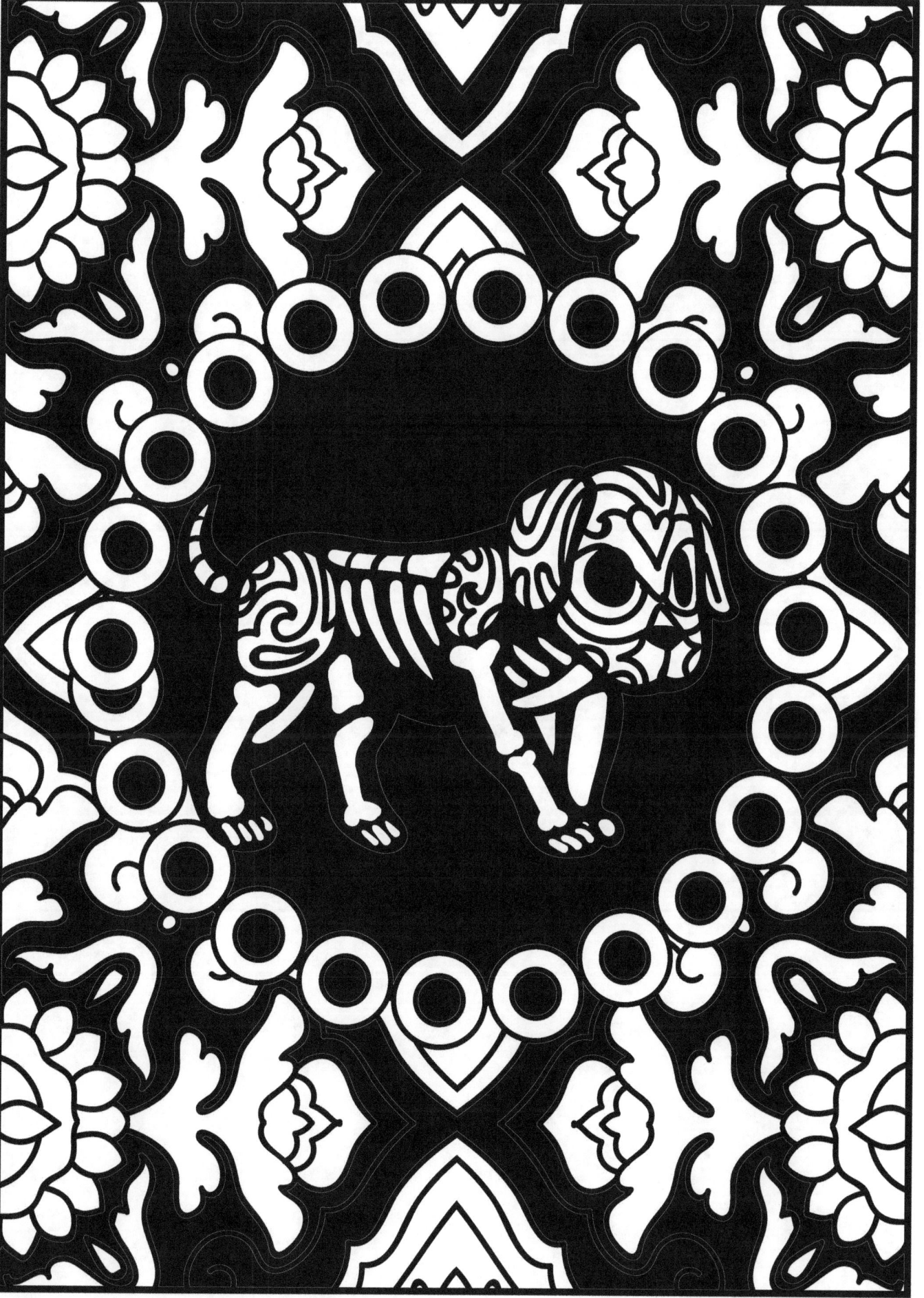

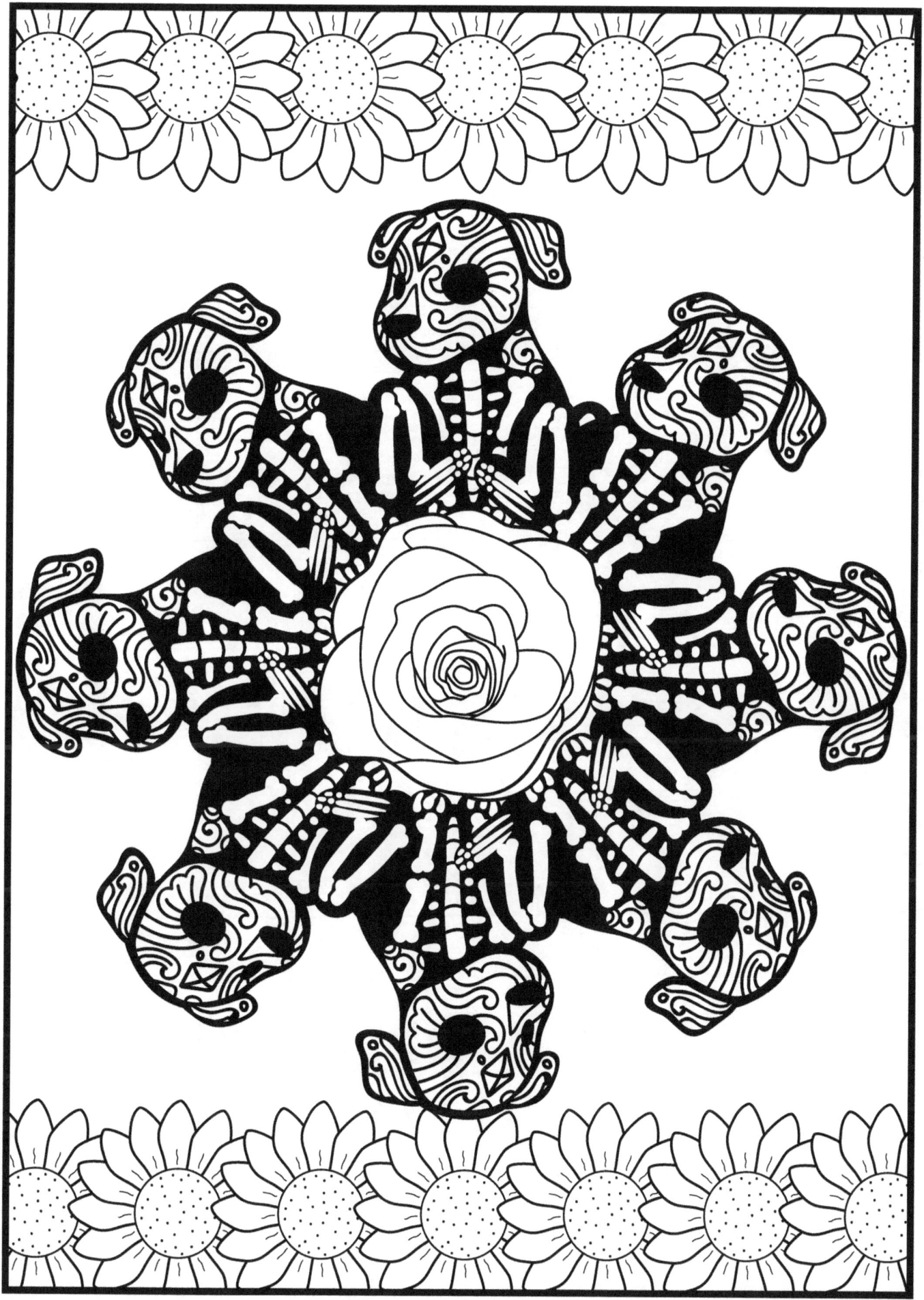

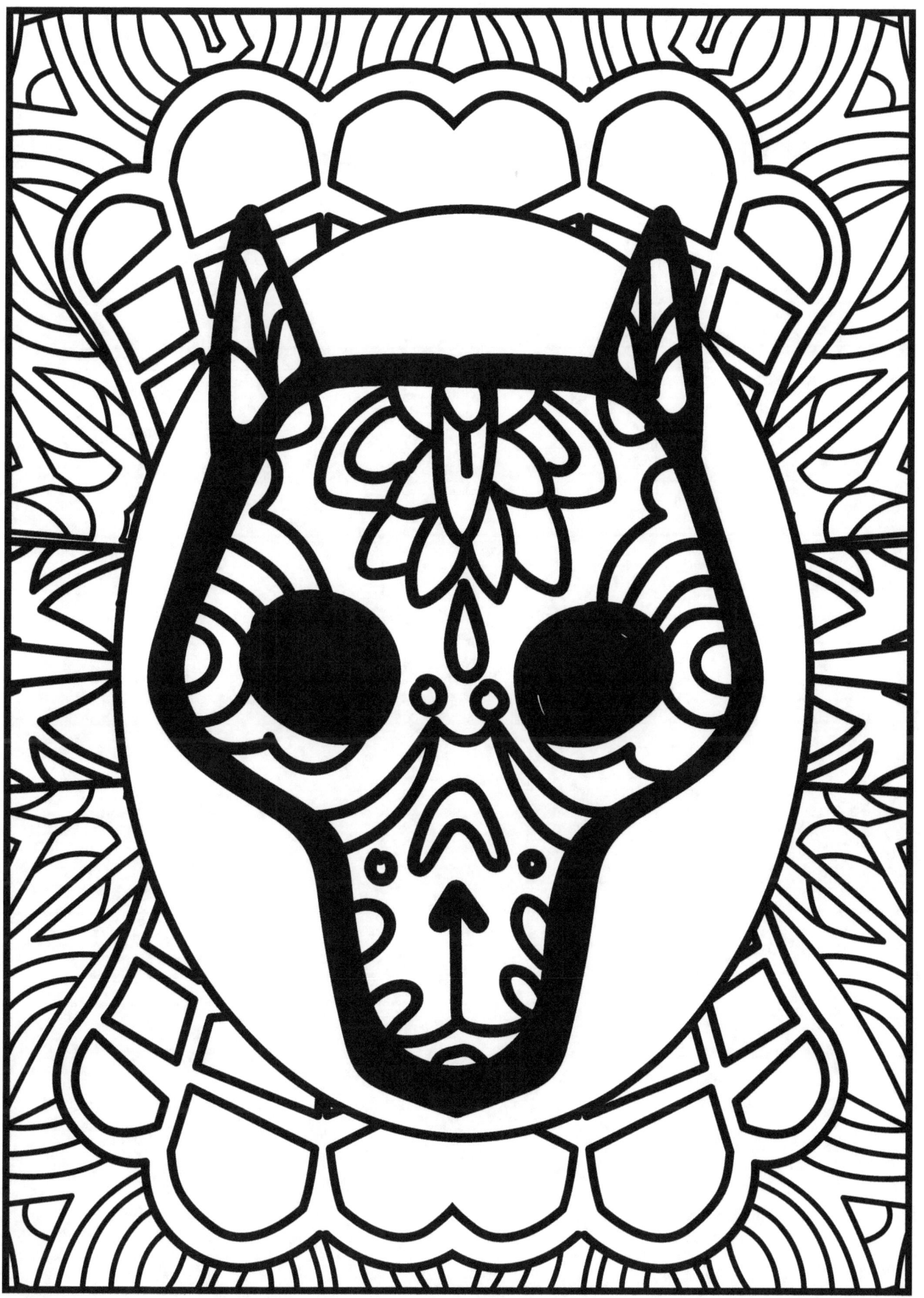

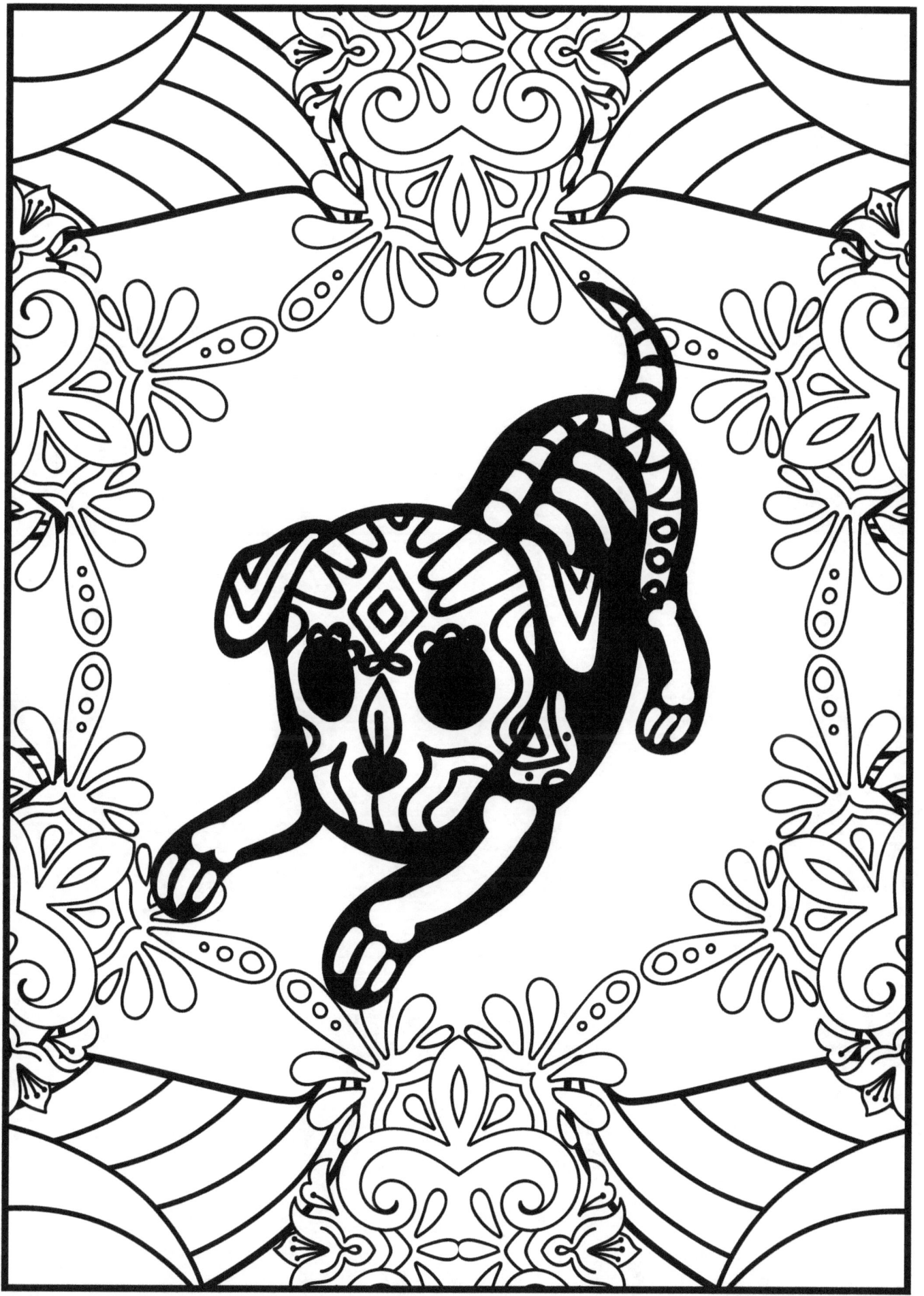

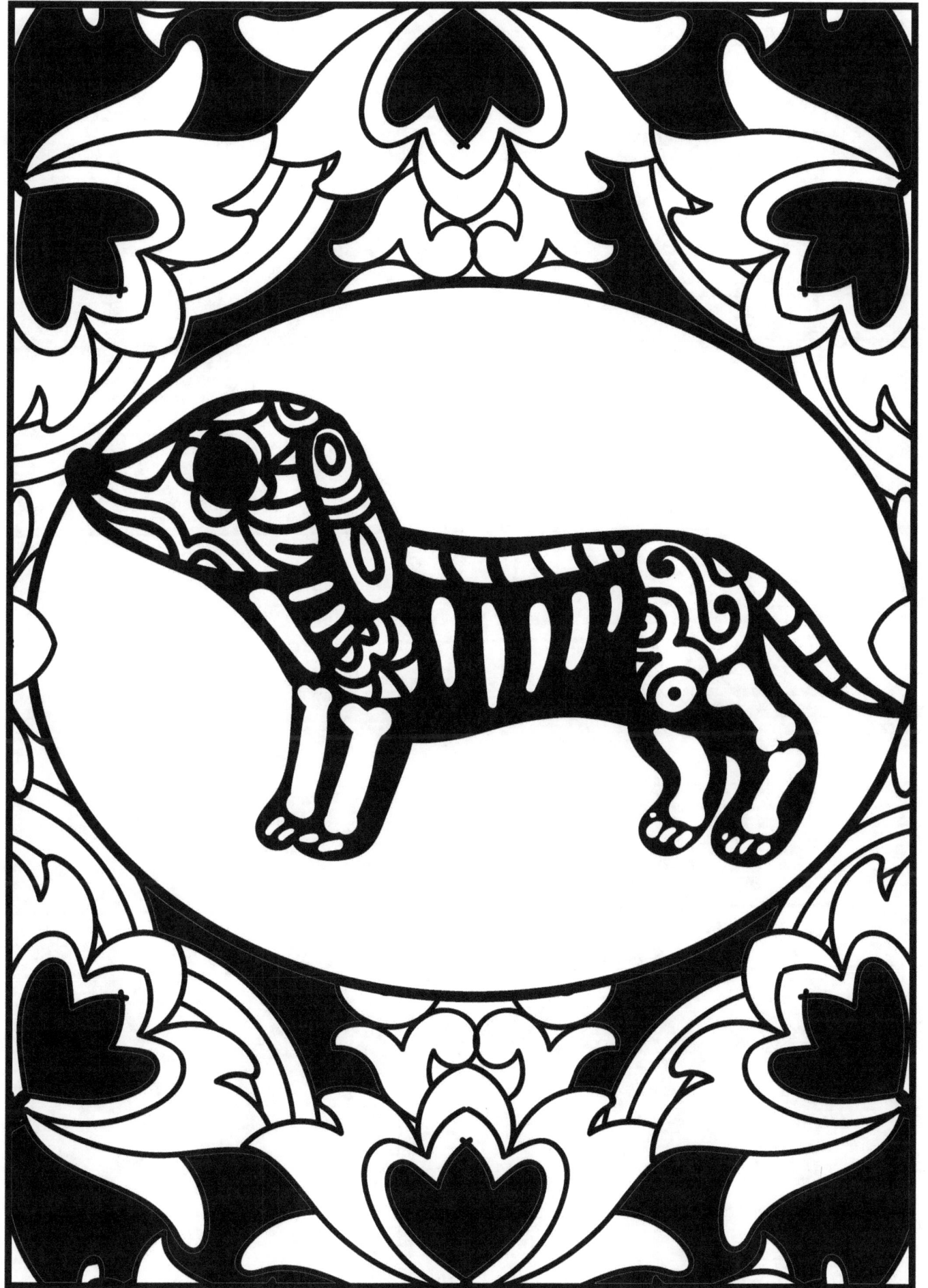

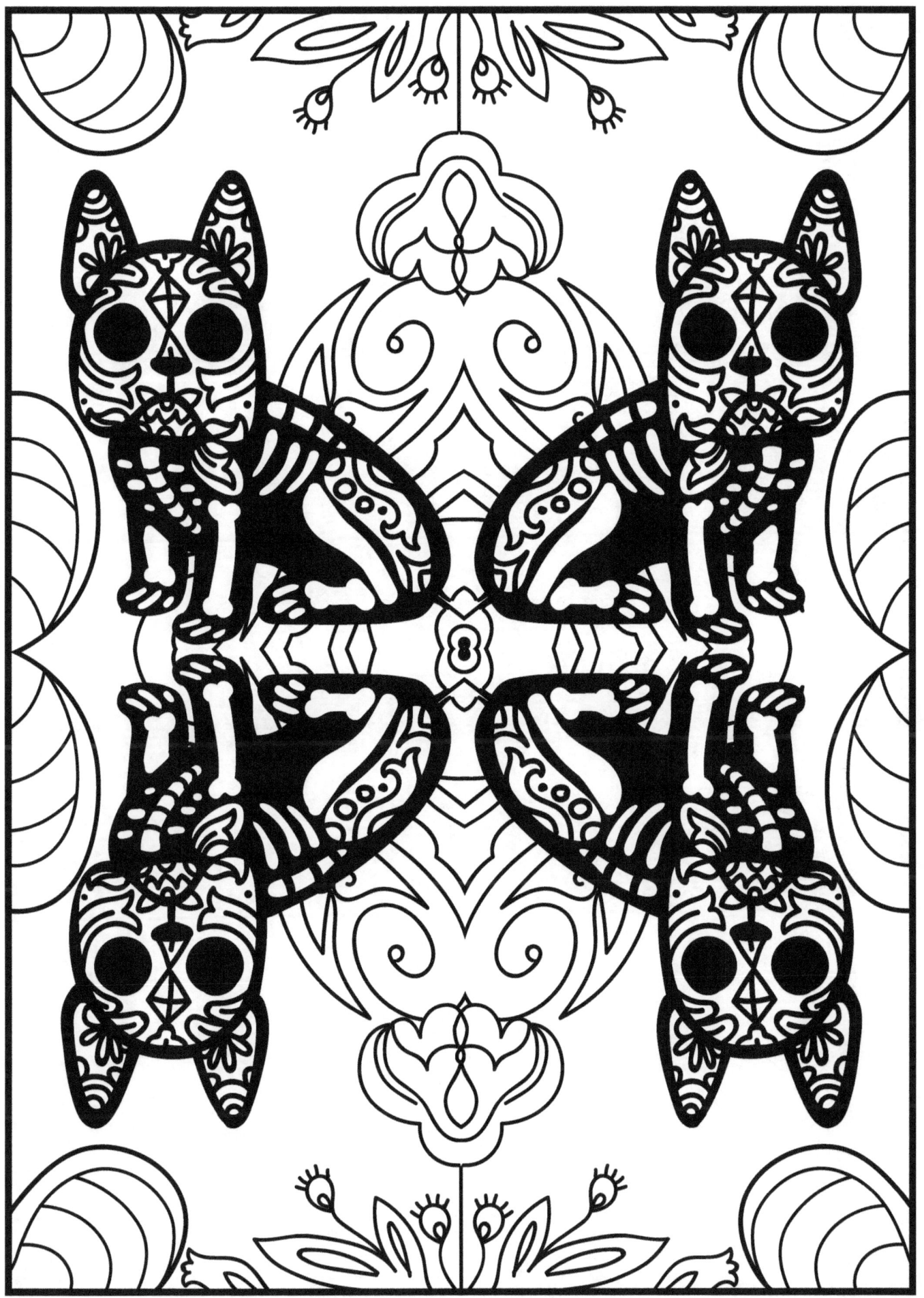

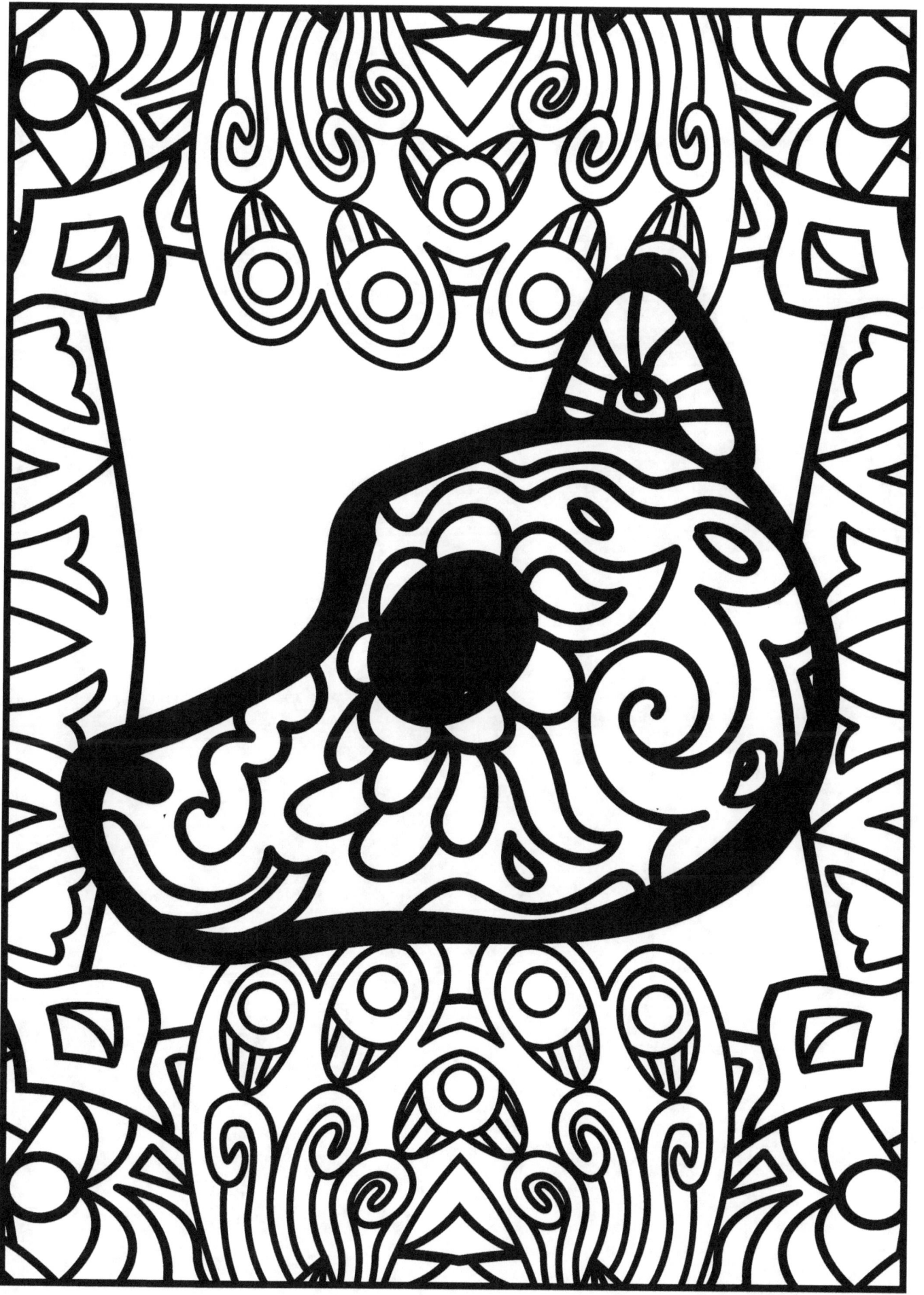

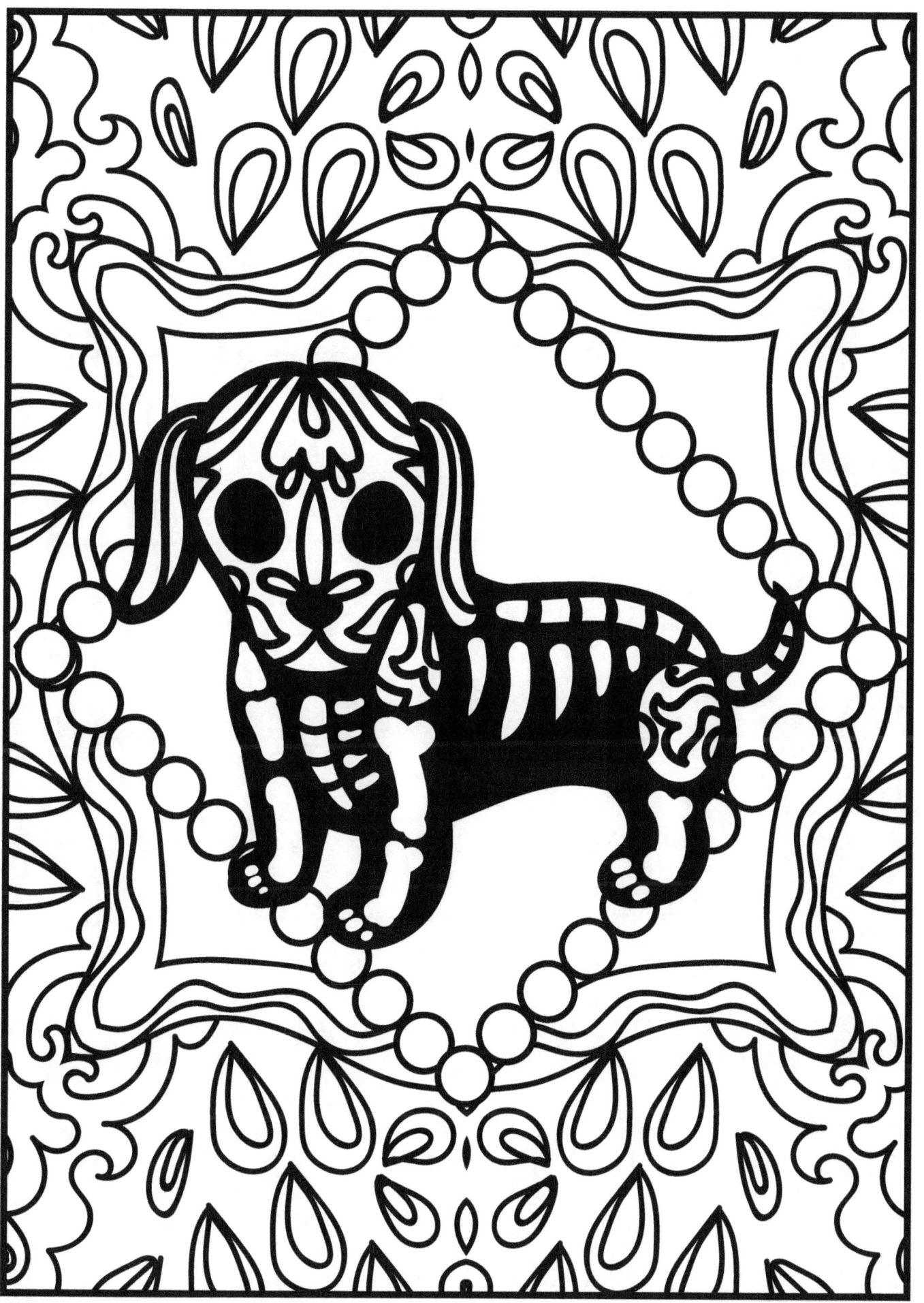

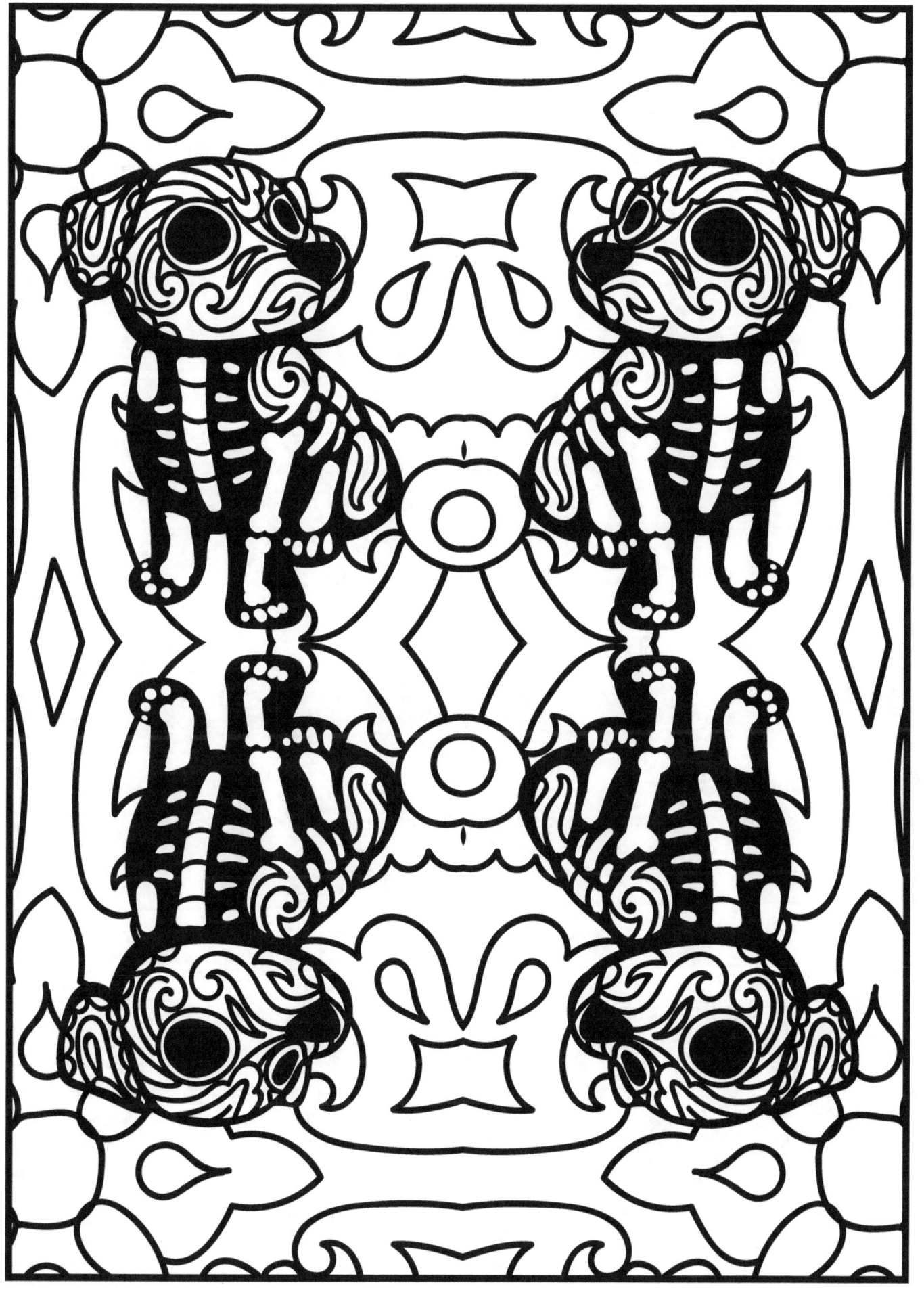

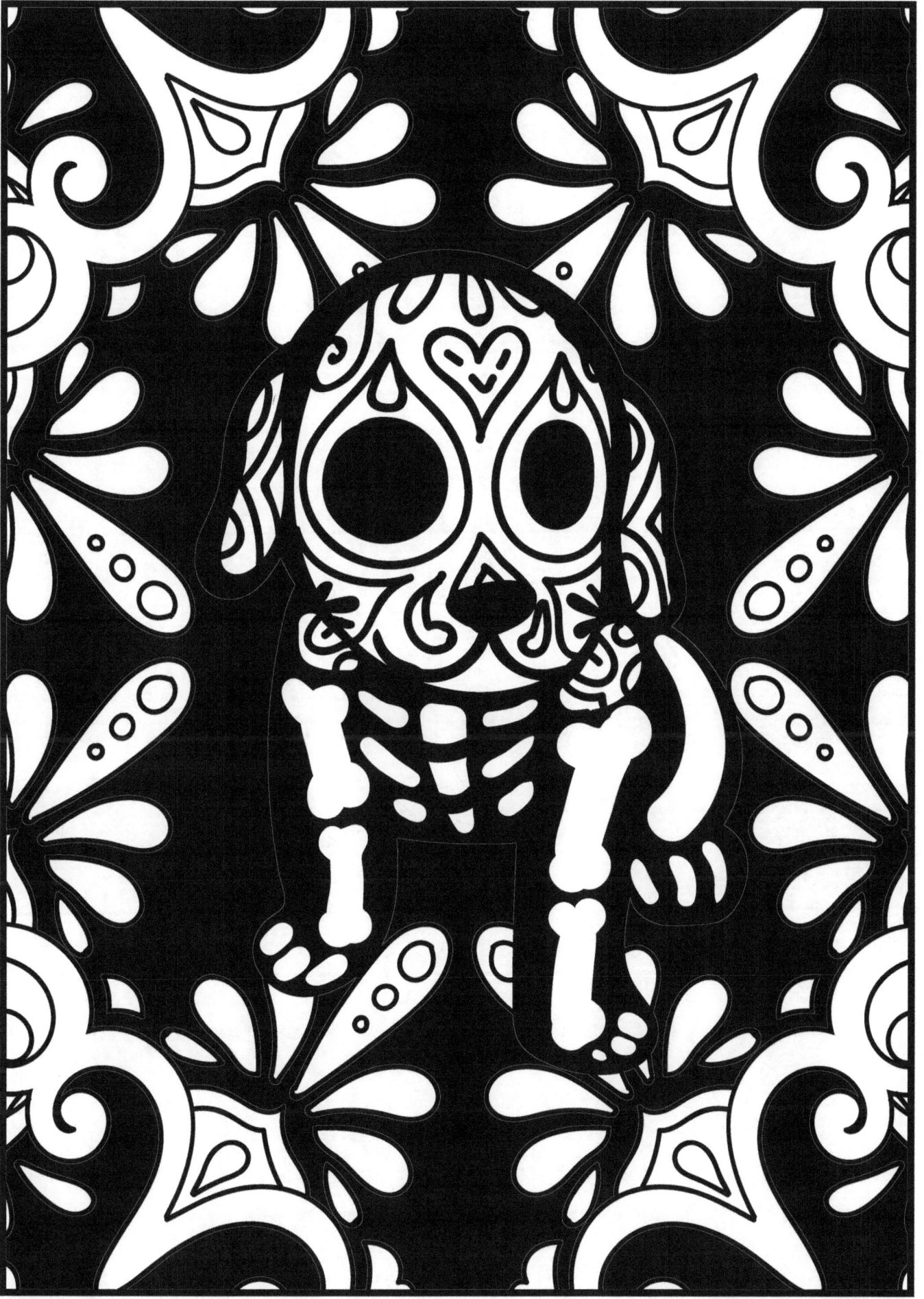

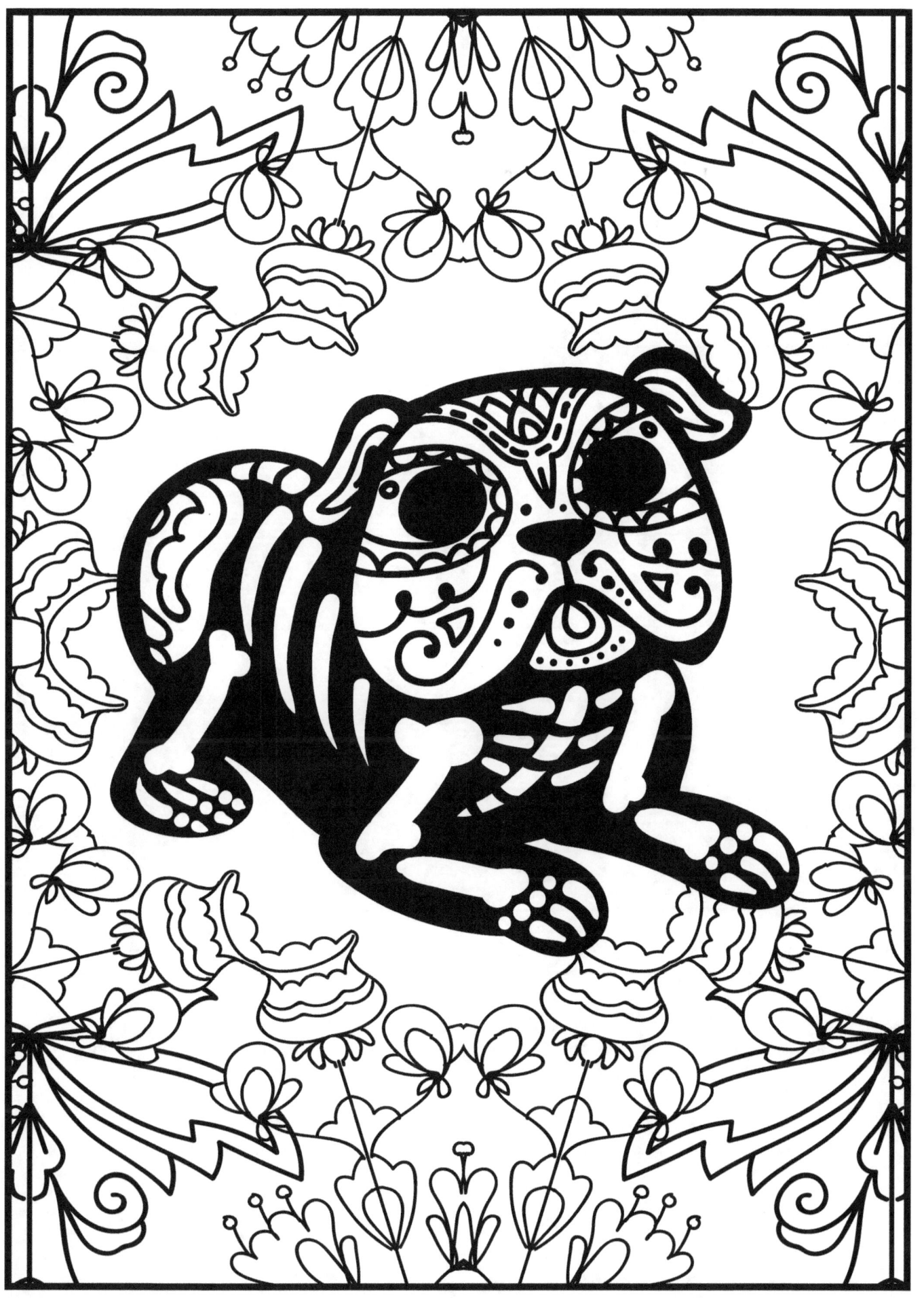

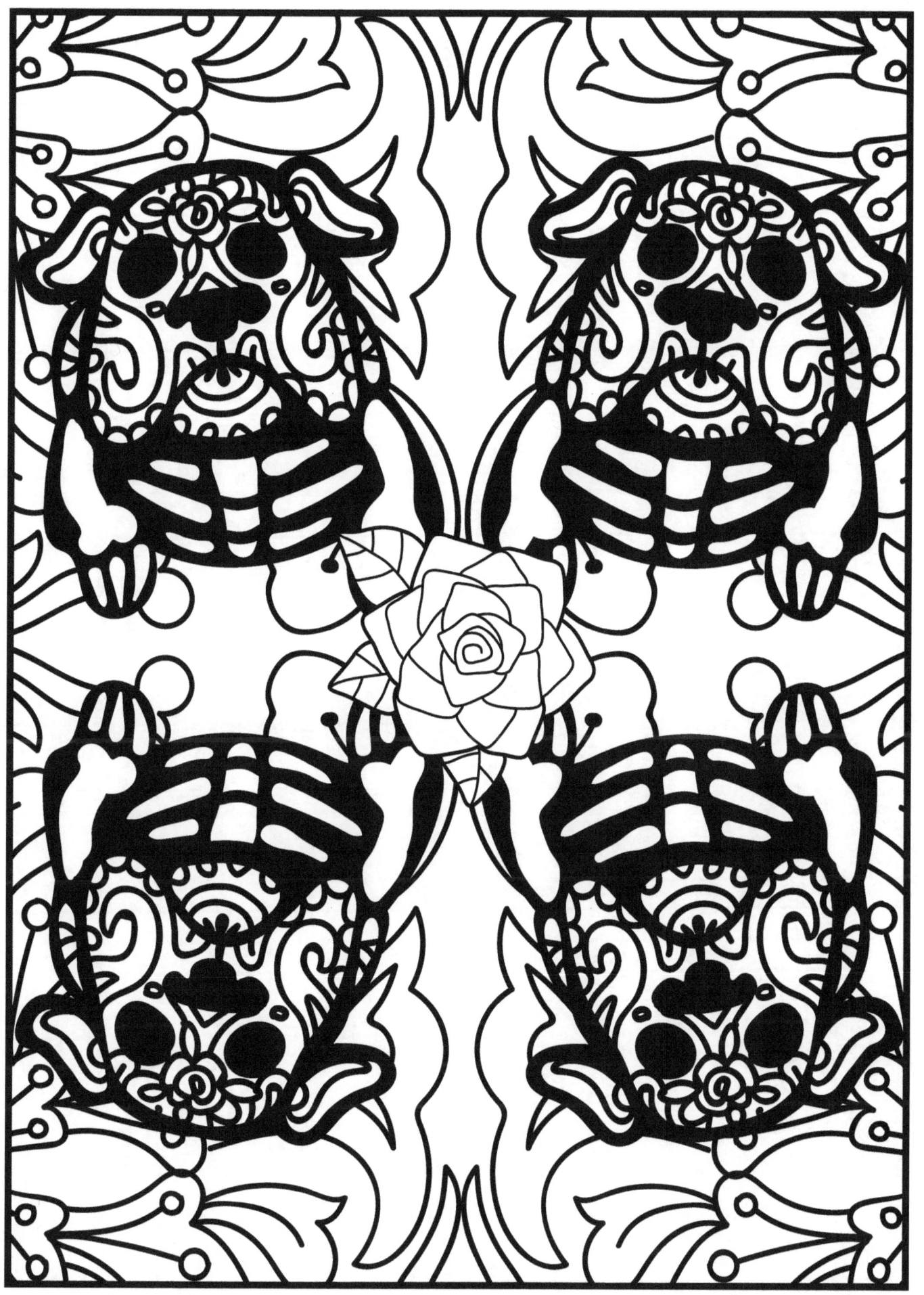

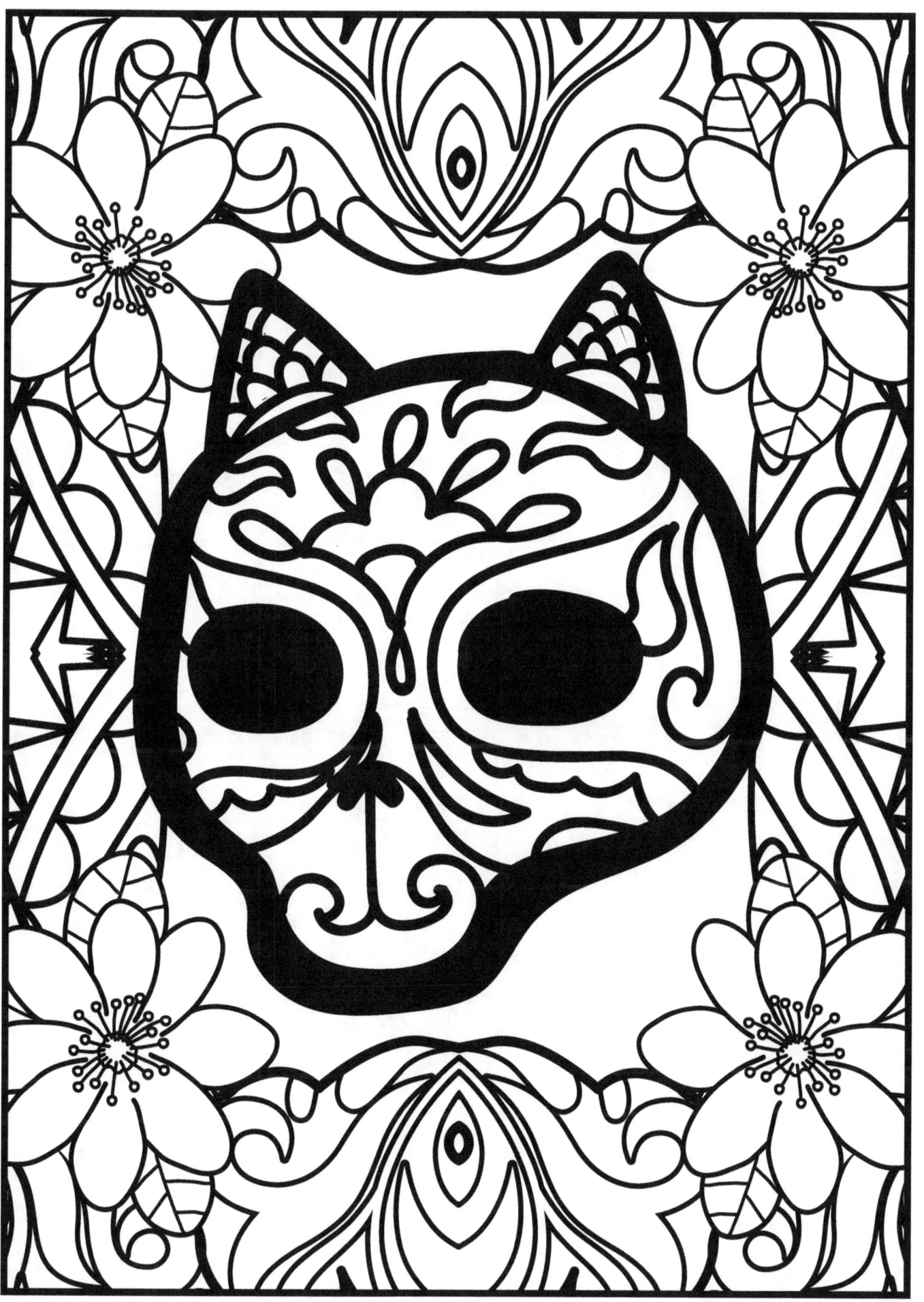

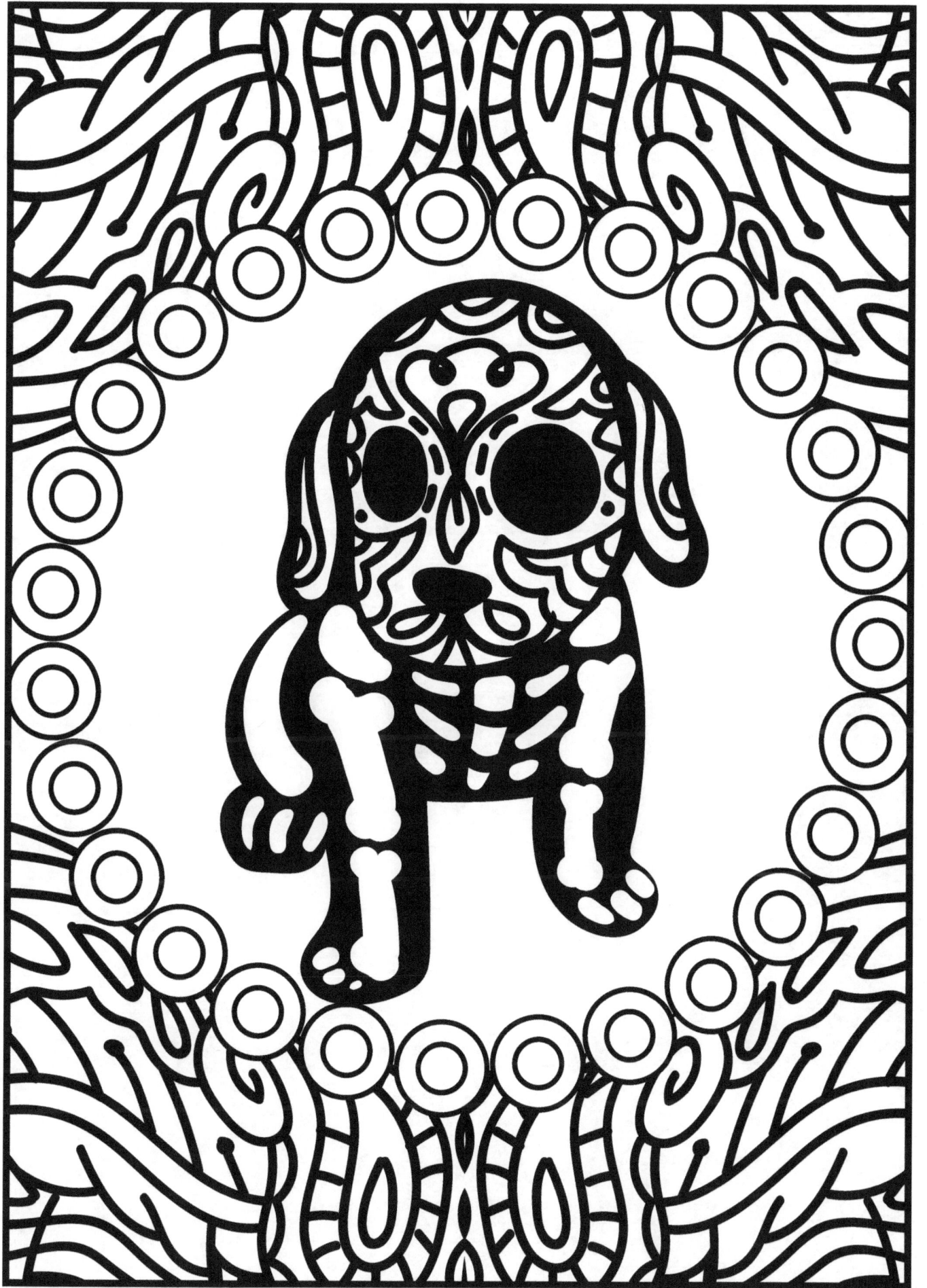

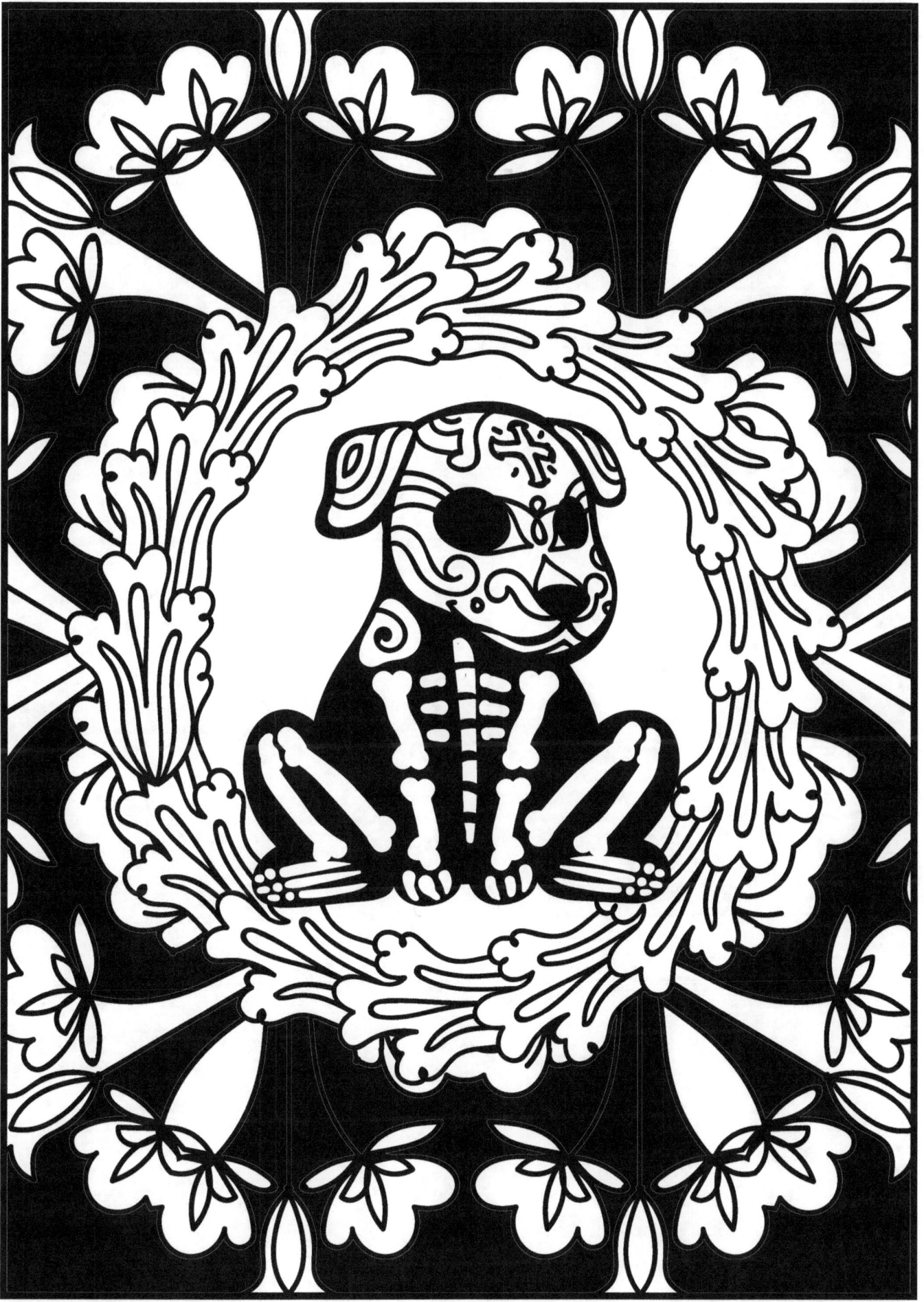

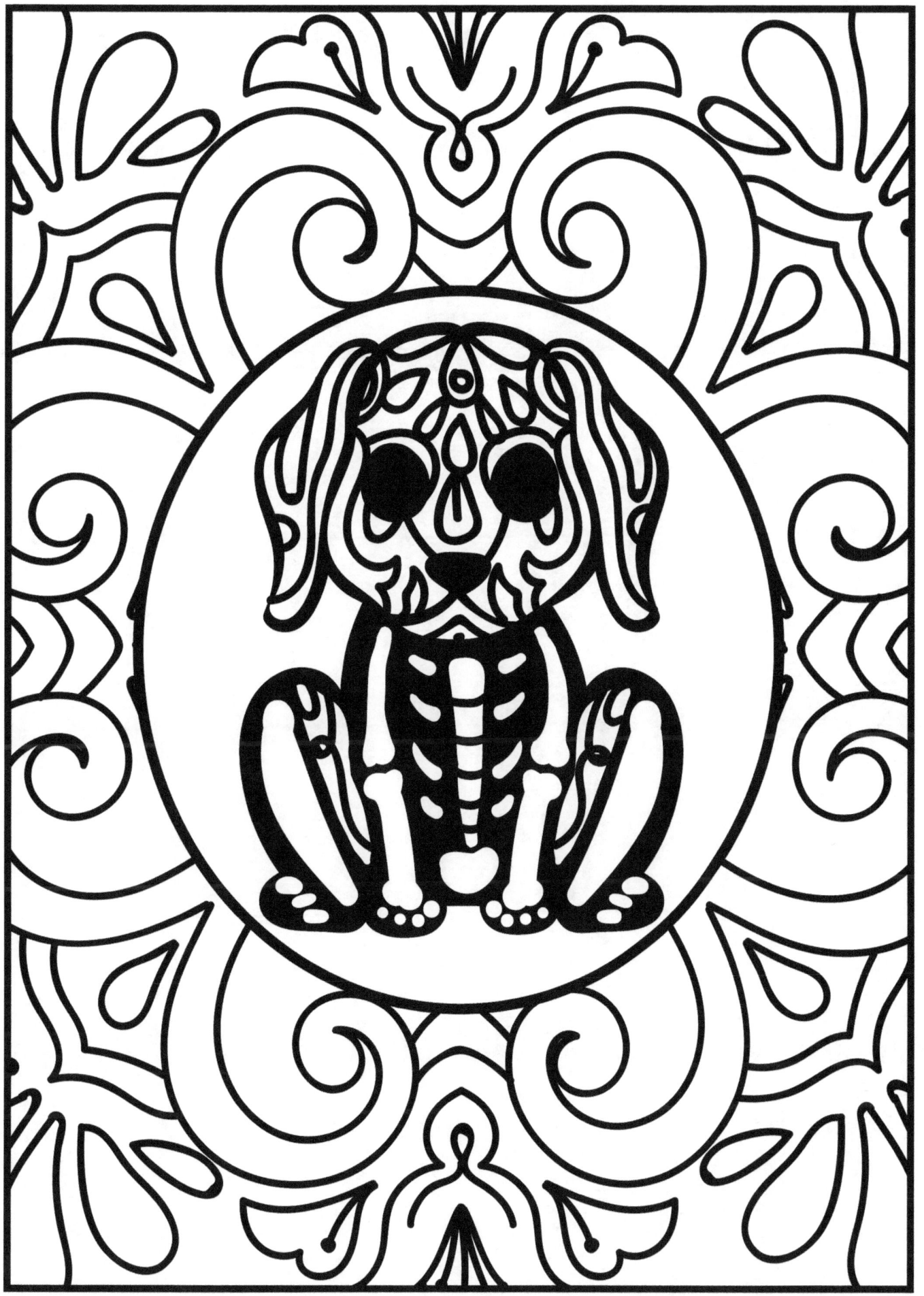

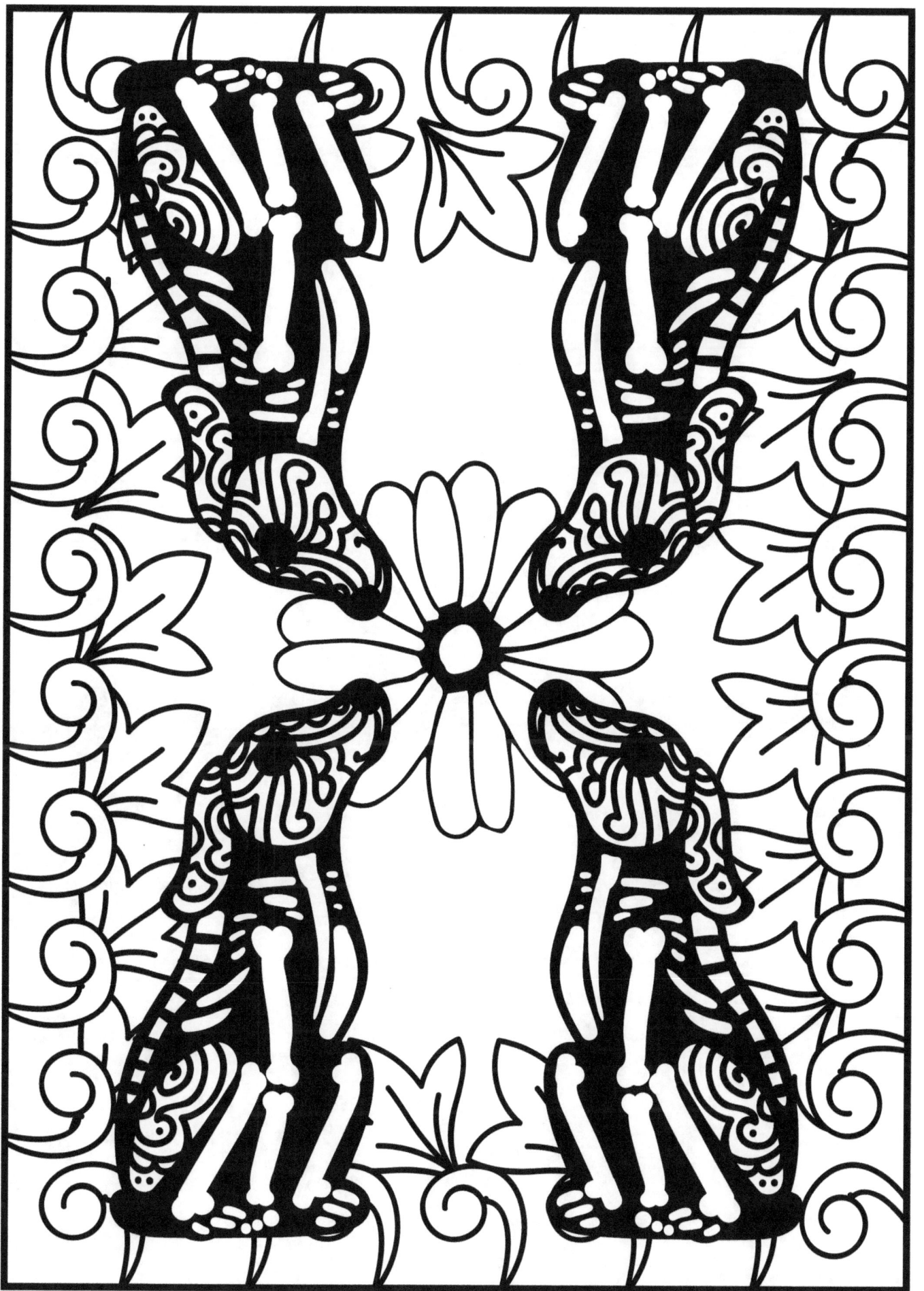

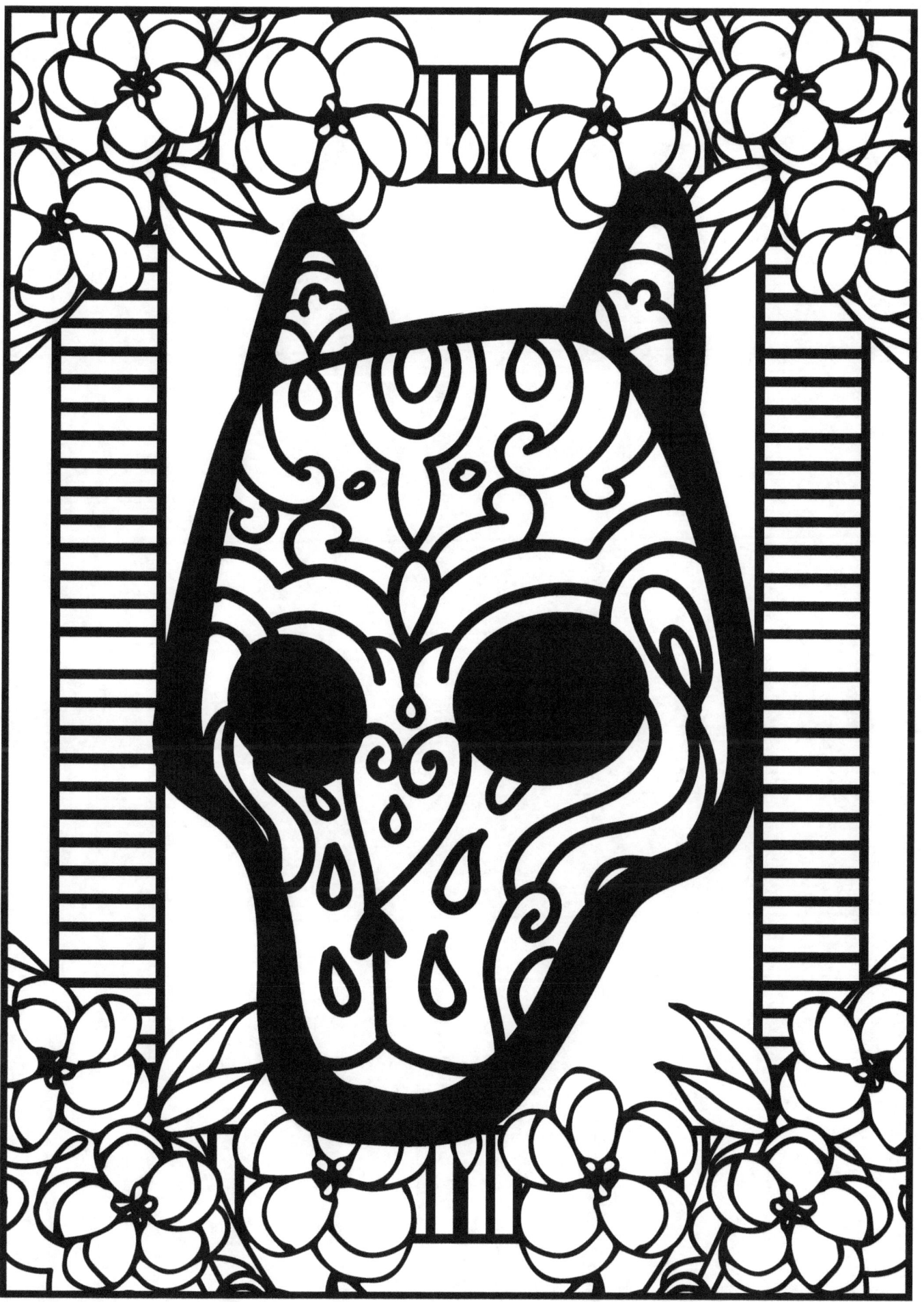

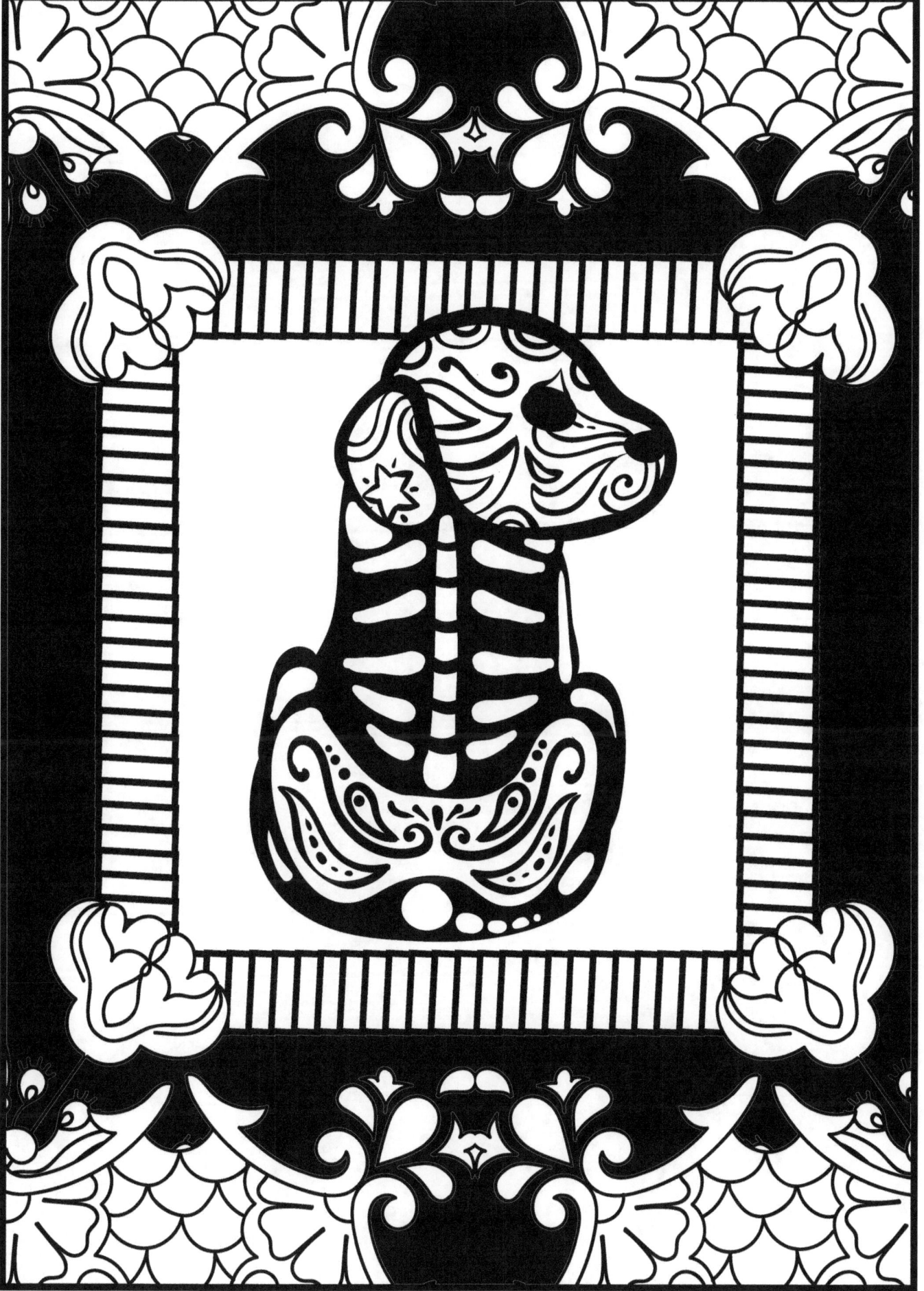

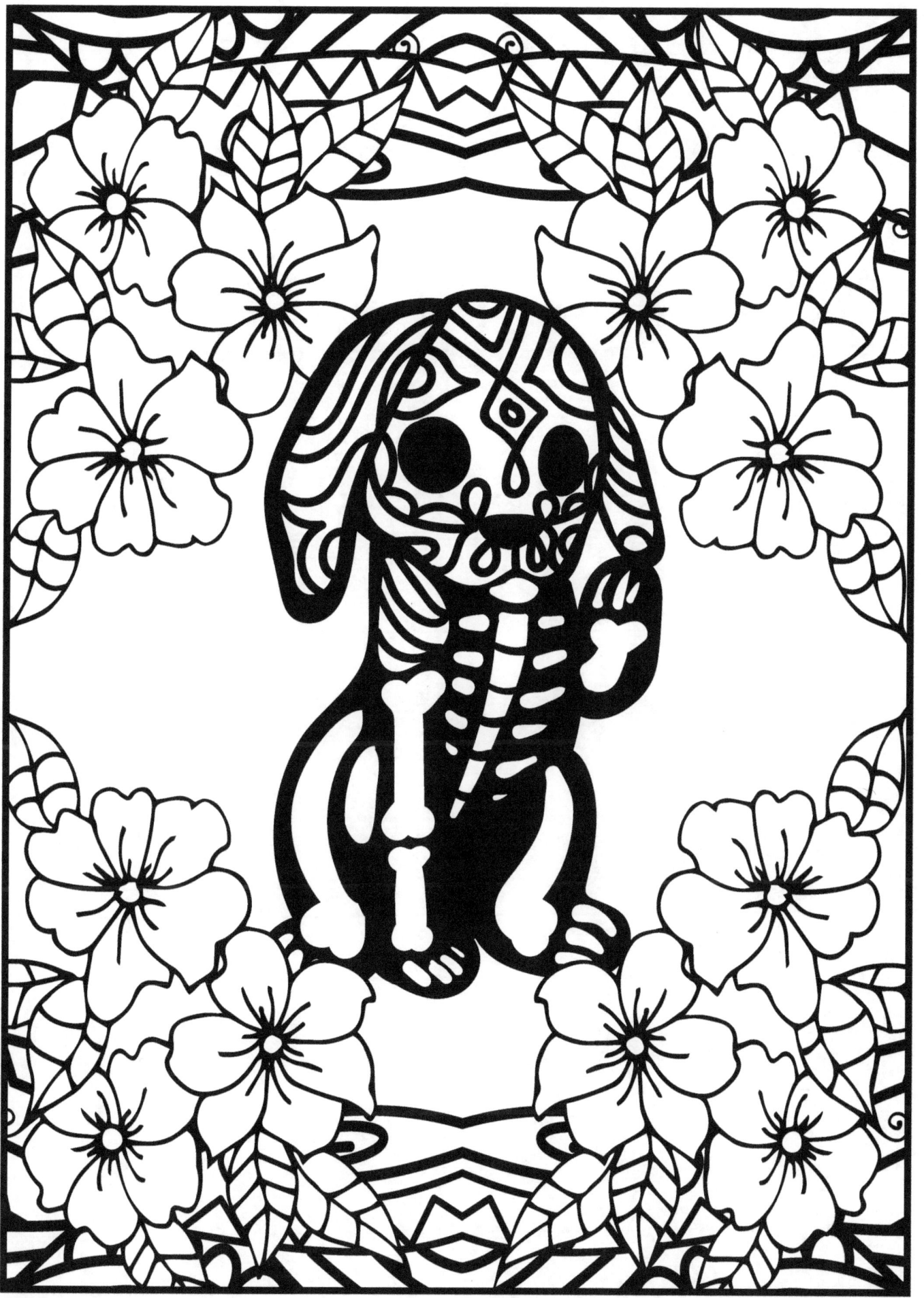

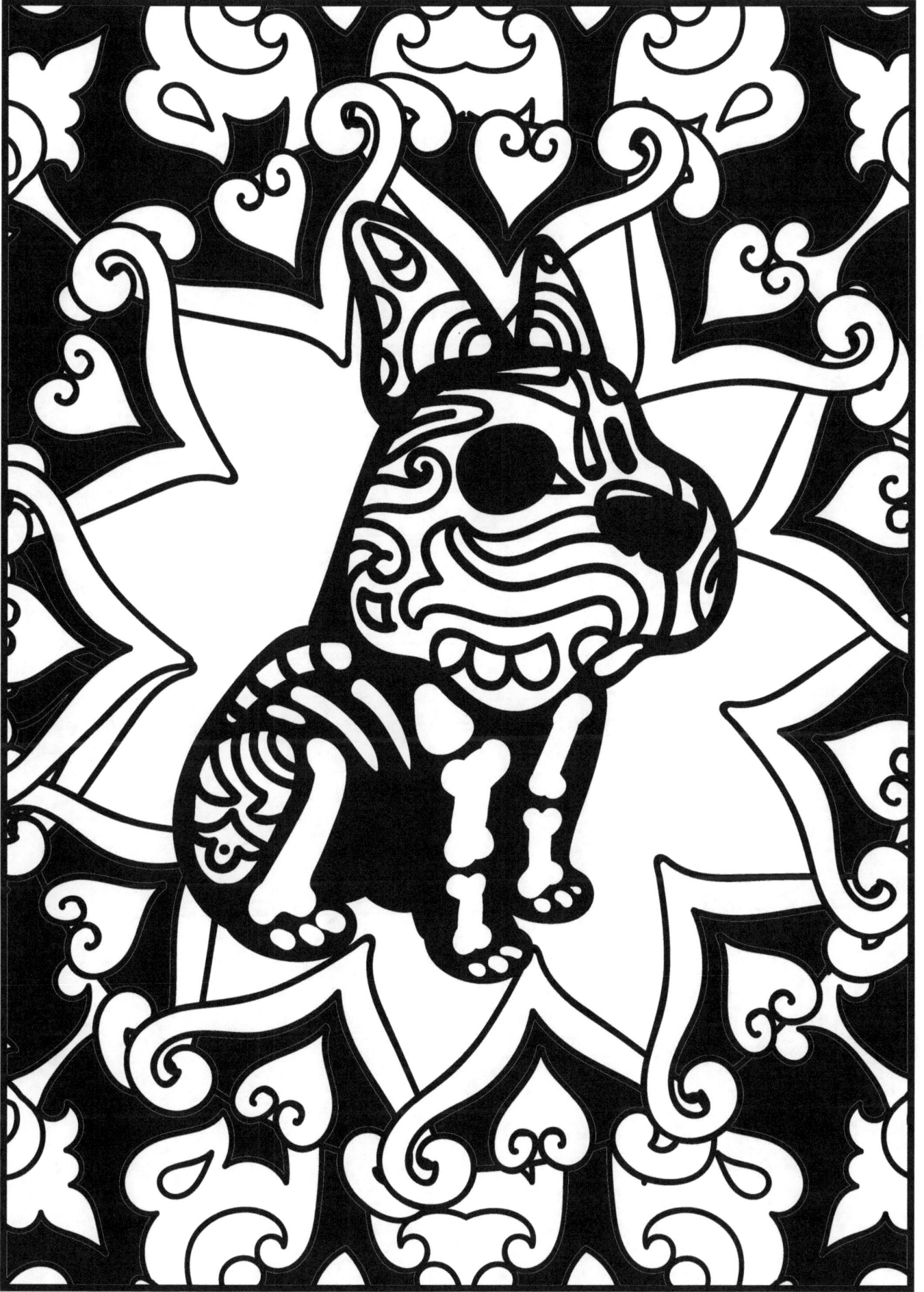

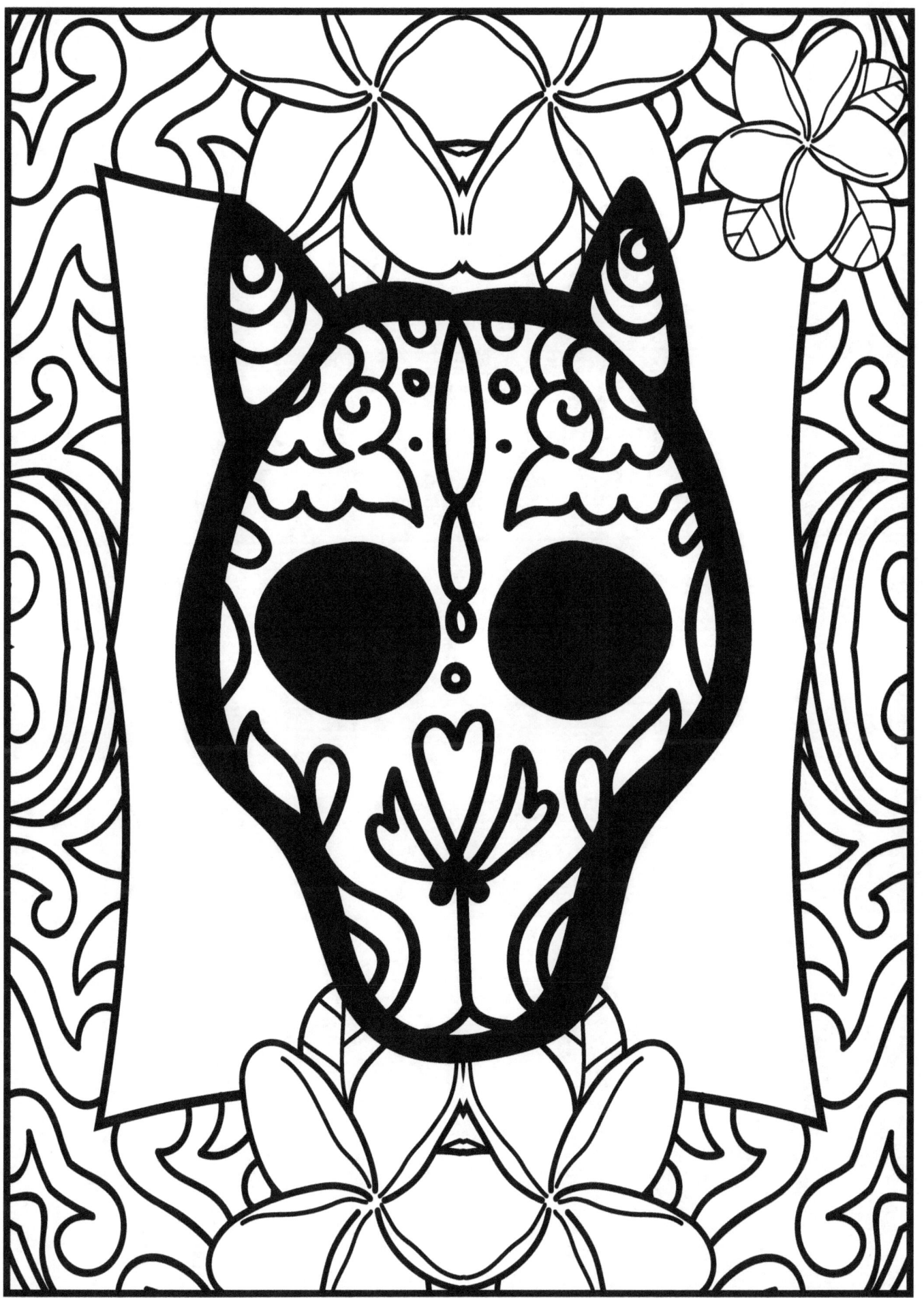

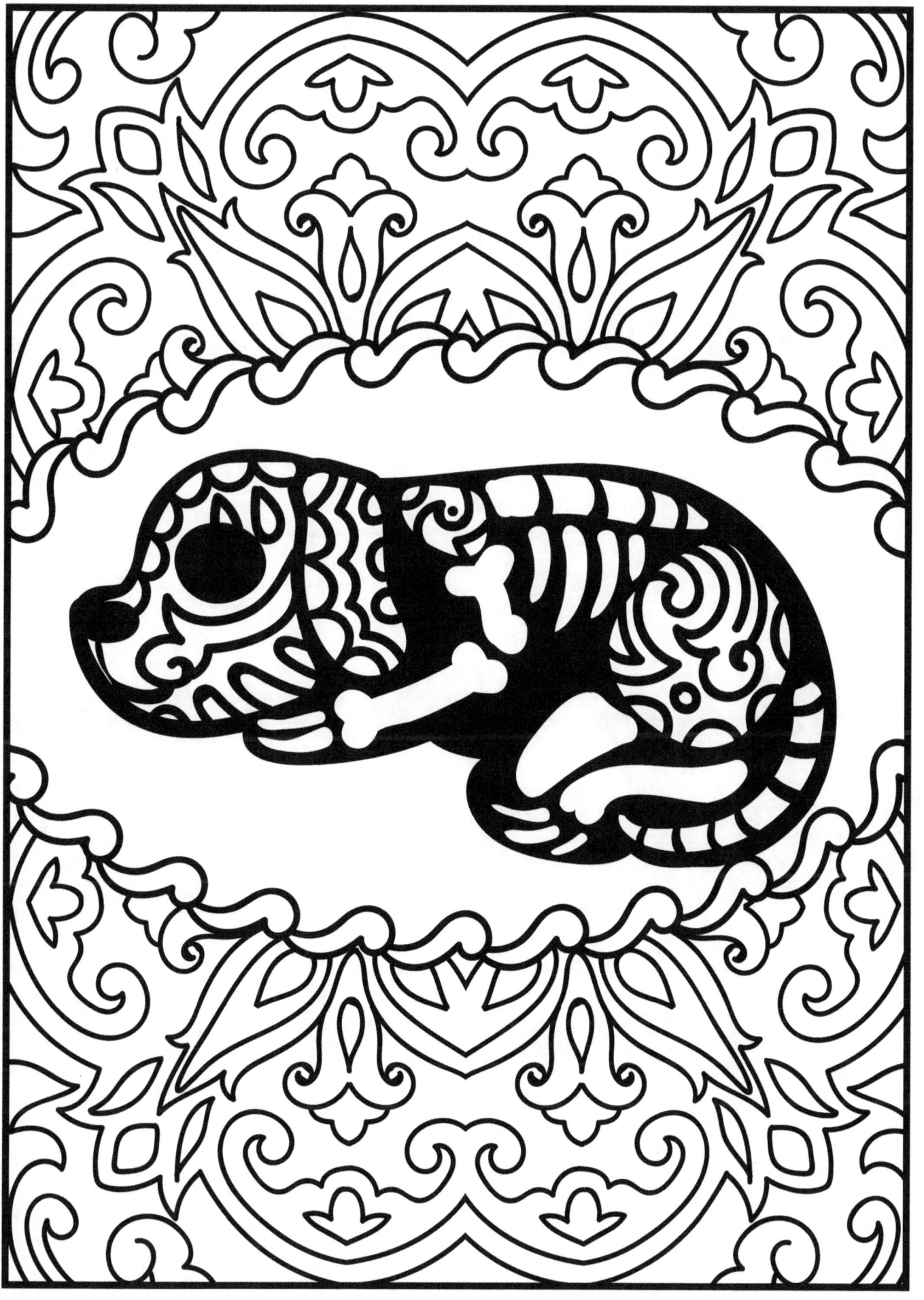

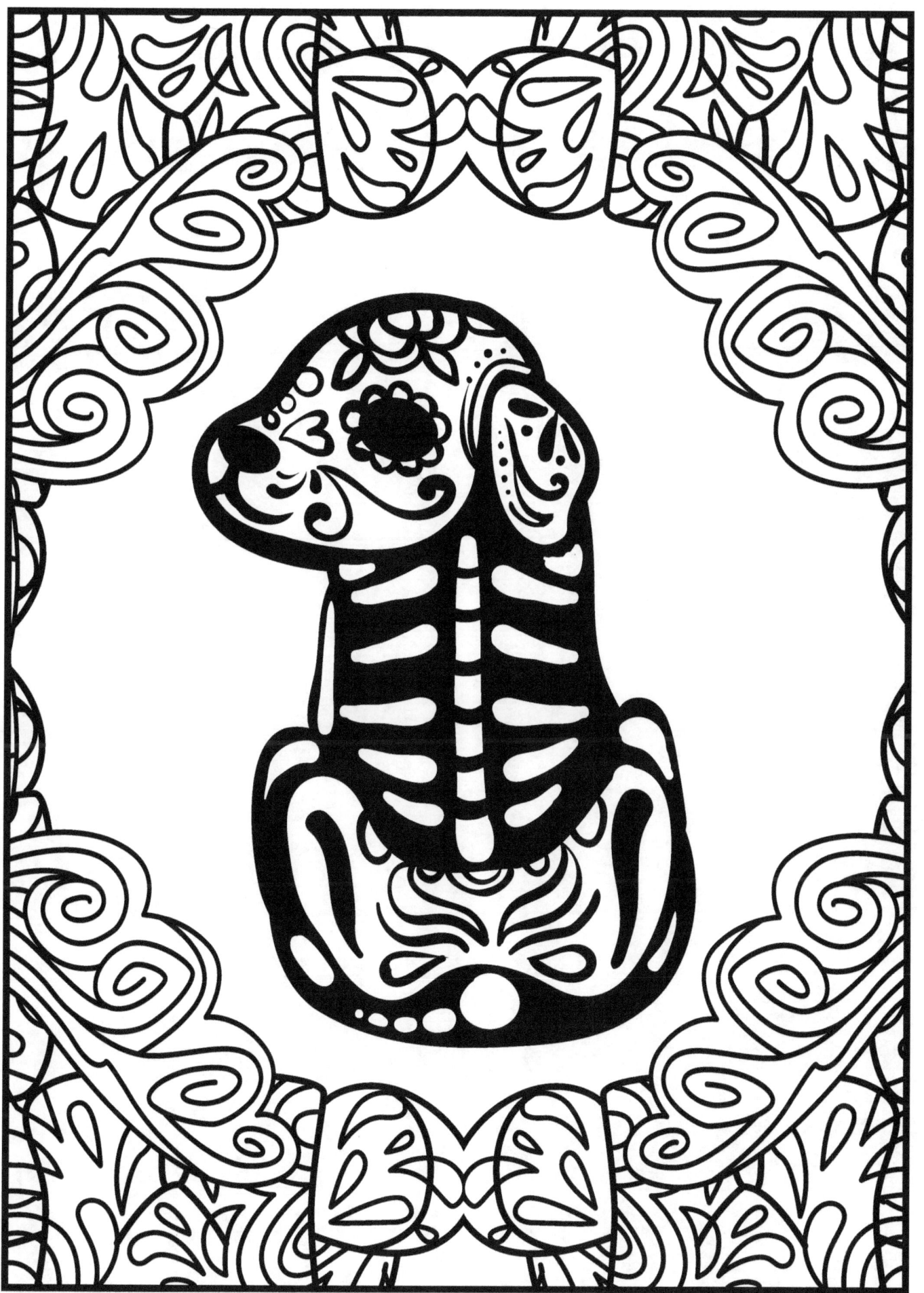

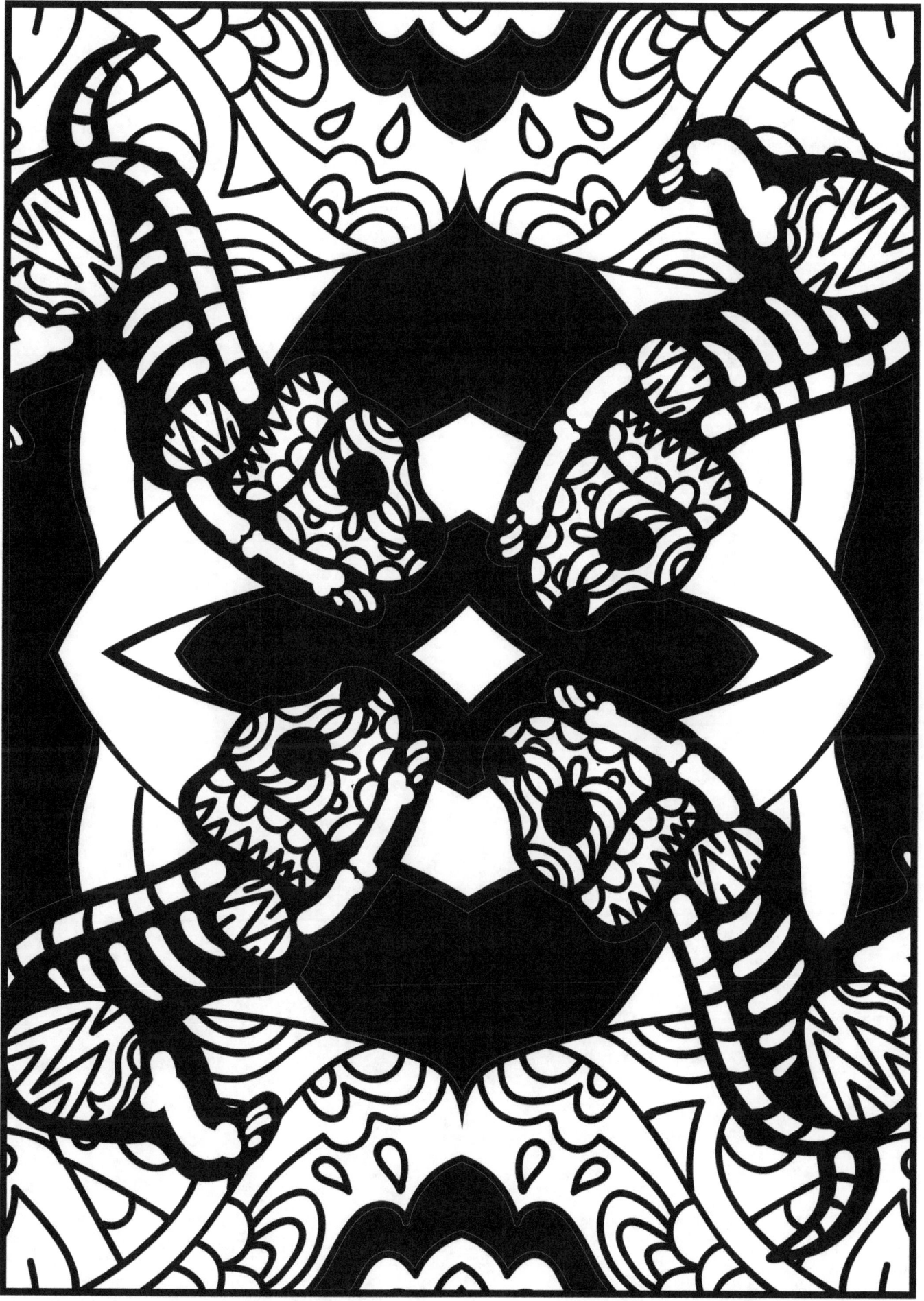

www.ingramcontent.com/pod-product-compliance
Lightning Source LLC
Chambersburg PA
CBHW080622190526
45169CB00009B/3262